Tony King

Off The Blocks

© 2013 Tony King. All rights reserved.
ISBN 978-1-291-47685-9

CONTENTS

FOREWORD		5
INTRODUCTION		7
Chapter 1.	SHAPING THE TEAM	11
Chapter 2.	FROM SHAPE TO SCULPTURE	43
Chapter 3.	FROM SCULPTURE TO MASTERPIECE	71
Chapter 4.	THE SCIENCE IN THE ART OF COACHING	123
Chapter 5.	THE ART IN THE SCIENCE OF COACHING	169
Chapter 6.	ME, YOU AND THEM	203
Chapter 7.	SUMMARY	235
Acknowledgements		239

Foreword

There are very few people who can say that they have coached youngsters, who went on to become top sports people, but whom have also coached and managed people in industry for over 30 years. There are probably fewer, who have seen the connection between the two types of coaching and sought to combine them, taking the best elements of Sports coaching and applying them to a business context. Career managers in industry can also have mixed and confused views on what coaching is let alone how to do it. There tends to be a gulf between the 'teachers' and mentors and the really good coaches.

What makes this particular take on the principle interesting is that it comes from one such manager; one who has also, co-incidentally, spent time as a sports coach. The power in such a view comes from the experience of real situations and real people in the workplace, not just a set of principles to be applied. The author has been there, seen how things work and is therefore able to translate the sports coaches thinking, with much more realism and credibility. Examples are real ones, taken from the workplace, not carefully constructed analogous stories to make a point. In that way, it is much easier for the reader to take the content away and use it almost immediately.

Neither is the author an acknowledged academic. Not that there is anything wrong with being an academic, it is just that, sometimes, it takes a holistic view based upon actual experience, rather than just gathering data and theorising, to really get to the heart of a subject. Coming at it from another angle, there are some Sports people now beginning to use their particular views on coaching and bring it to the business forum. Having been coached, continually, for many years, the Sports stars can quite easily see why business coaching doesn't really have the same bite. It is negatively charged and often sporadic, making it appear that it is a 'tick in the box' exercise, rather than something done for the good of the coachee or the team.

So what makes this book different? What makes the authors view relevant and easy to put into practice? It is simple. You don't need complex diagrams or theories, you just need two things; to have seen, participated in or appreciated a sport and be able to draw a comparison from the sport to a particular situation in business. Some sports lend themselves to the business context better than others

Thanks must go to a few other people too for their advice, inspiration, input and guidance in the vision and execution of this book.

I would like therefore to thank;

Professor Patrick Duffy at Leeds Metropolitan University, whose courses on Coaching for Performance were inspirational and whose encouragement in the initial stages of this project was beneficial.

Andrew Edwards, Radio Leeds Presenter, who was enthusiastic and complimentary on a few sample pages early in the books evolution.

My son Martin King, for his sterling work in Coaching Wing Chung students. His methods and analogies when teaching complex moves are memorable and insightful and helped me to think about the concepts I employ.

Introduction

"There'll be two buses leaving the hotel for the park tomorrow. The two o'clock bus will be for those of you who need a little extra work. The empty bus will leave at five o'clock." David Bristol, Milwaukee Brewers manager.

If you are a manager in any industry, you will be frequently bombarded with literature, information on courses and general wisdom on how to be a better manager. Most of it is the same or very similar in content. There are always lists of things you should try to do more of and, as you might expect, a list of things you really should avoid doing.

I was always glad of those little tips, hints and reminders. I would never have worked them out for myself. Like most people I thought that I was a reasonably good manager. I had a couple of great pieces of advice from my father and one of my first bosses. '*Never ask anyone to do anything you wouldn't do yourself,*' and, '*Know your people.*' They are both frighteningly good in terms of their simplicity and context. However, in this complicated world, it is never quite enough to have just two tenets. There are a plethora of things you *must* learn and implement, that the best have brought to us, neatly packaged, tried and tested; but enough of my sarcasm and cynicism.

If these processes are so amazing, why aren't we all getting the very best; the last drop; the actual essence out of our people? Why are there people like myself, who have felt the need to put digits to keyboard to produce yet another guide on the subject? Simple, most of the others are too complicated to implement. They sound great; they even work, to a degree. They make an awful lot of sense, but there is just something a little corny and trite about most of them. They are almost too obvious when you try to implement them and the whole thing starts to look like an exercise rather than something that you feel and that your team will feel is natural and very much a part of what you are about. Some of the other less complex ones are just, well, too simple to be effective. Theorise as much as you like, you are dealing with a very complex organism. When that organism interacts with other equally complex organisms you cannot always predict the outcome.

So, the situation is not that simple, neither is it blindingly complex, and yet people have been doing it effectively for centuries, it is the answer you have been searching for and it will make you a better manager, but you are not ready for it yet.

First, you have to examine what it is that you actually want to do. Do you want to improve your standing as a Manager? Are you trying to impress someone? Do you really only want to learn how to improve the people who report to you and develop them? The contents in the following pages are aimed to let you achieve the latter, but it will do the other two as a matter of course.

The answer is actually all about sports coaching, but represented slightly differently and put into the business context. Think about it. A sports coach takes a person, or a team, with talent and gets the best performance out of them. How they do that; how they get people to perform and succeed is not some sort of magic formula or complicated theory. It's simply about people. As long as you understand the principles of what it is they, and you, are trying to achieve, you can coach someone to achieve it. In the case of great sports coaches, quite often, they may have been sportspeople themselves who have moved into coaching and achieved even more as coaches. Many end up making some of their charges more successful than they ever were, or ever could be. You may wonder how or why that is possible. The answer lies within.

Trying to follow the previously prescribed methods of business coaching in the environment I worked in, was a little like trying to paddle a canoe with one of the little spoons you get with an Ice Cream tub at the Theatre. It was the right shape; it was made of the right material, but it was designed for something utterly different. I began to use my own sports coaching experience to help me come up with the right approach. It was all about a defined sequence and a sustained and planned approach rather than a gimmick or a few buzz words, anachronisms or phrases.

Don't get me wrong, but many of these cure-all approaches have been written by academics who, may have never worked on the shop floor and experienced the horrors of not just bad, but cruel and vindictive management. They have theorised based upon what they have observed remotely and what they perceive *should be* the right way. It is a little like people used to believe that the moon was made of cheese, just because it looked a little bit cheese-like.

So, being one of those who knew the Moon was actually a big spherical rock and that most of the stuff already written was, shall we say, utopian, I decided I had to write my own version. Hopefully, you will find it absolutely priceless and more importantly, relevant to all your situations.

Coaching, in any context, is not about being trite or superficial. It contains elements of psychology, technical knowledge, detailed observation, deconstruction and reconstruction and a number of other necessary components. As the quote at the head of this introduction suggests, we are none of us without the scope to improve ourselves and those in our charge. If we are all prepared to accept that we are not perfect; that we can and want to be improved, then coaching has to be the way to achieve that.

It is also essential to know what coaching is not. It is not training. It is not teaching. You may coach during a training session, you may teach during a coaching session, but do not confuse these development methods.

One other reason for writing this guide is that I have a very strong impulse to share my findings and the revelations which inspired me. If we all improve, and our coaching collectively improves, everybody will ultimately benefit. Businesses will benefit; individuals will benefit and people who would otherwise be left to their own devices will be given the attention and input they deserve. I reckon that is a good enough reason to start with.

CHAPTER 1.

SHAPING THE TEAM

"Business is more exciting than any game." **Lord Beaverbrook**

In this chapter we explore who and what it is we are coaching. The basics of coaching are all about the shape, the dynamic, who we are coaching and the key objectives which make up what we are ultimately aiming for. This could be aiming to produce a great swimmer, golfer, runner or footballer. In our sphere of interest it is about developing a business person. It could be you, one of your team, a manager or director. The point is that you have to know and understand a number of key principles before you start to coach. A swimming coach can't just be dragged in, off the street, and be expected to coach a swimmer. They need at the very least two things. These are; a rudimentary knowledge of swimming and knowledge of how to coach swimmers. What are the key points? What are the objectives? What makes for good technique? Another key area is the environment or the medium we are coaching in. Is it a pool or open water? In business is it a private or public company, is it a Government department? All of these will have a bearing on how we coach and what we focus on.

In shaping the team, we also need to look at the basics of pulling together a coaching plan. This involves choosing the correct starting point, and then in looking at the next step, the triggers involved in making the work begin to fly and, of course, the dynamics. These could be the dynamics of the environment, the people, the team or the relationship between you and them.

Shaping the team is about starting correctly and setting the foundations. Once these principles are entrenched, then the real coaching can start; on that additional detail, refinement and finesse.

The sub-sections in this and subsequent chapters build in sequence and are therefore best read that way. Just a coaching point!

1.1. Getting the head right

In quite a lot of sports, the position of the head is important to the body shape, the stance; the execution of movement or the dynamics of the sport. If that positioning is wrong, quite often, those other things don't work how they should.

Consider Golf. If you address the ball, looking down at it when you swing and maintain that head position, you will strike the ball, as you intended, most of the time. Lift your head, or try to look where the ball is going during the swing, before you have actually made contact with it, and the shot will, more often than not, be a disaster.

In swimming, the position of the head determines the position of the body in the water. Starting with and keeping the head in the correct position eliminates zigzag, or lateral movement, feet and legs being too low and a whole bunch of other things which prevent optimum speed and efficiency being attained.

In association football, keeping your head over the ball when striking it will keep it low, leaning back will cause it to rise. We've all seen those disastrous penalties, hit sweetly into row twenty five of the stand.

So, we've established the first principle that, in a number of sports, if you get the head wrong, the end result is inevitably flawed. Now I know what you are thinking. How do we convert what part the head plays in sport, to what part the head plays in terms of management and coaching in business? It's a good question, but we can break it down.

In Golf, the head being still, helps bring the club head back to the starting point and through it, ensuring a clean contact. By keeping the head still, the swing brings everything back to the same place, even though the shoulders, arms and upper body are swinging around through a hundred and eighty degrees. It is all about stability and consistency.

In Swimming, it's all about the dynamics, keeping the body position straight and flat in the water to eliminate drag.

In football, it's about the angle at which the final contact between foot and ball is made, like a golf clubs pitch. It's about control.

So, what we are looking at is consistency, stability, control and dynamics.

These are the keys to looking at the 'head'.

In management terms, examine and analyse what attributes you have in individuals and in teams. How consistent is a person in the way they approach their tasks? Is it clear that they have a favourite task or tasks and other activities which are less-favourite? Do they tend to delegate or pass these off to someone else?

How stable are they? I don't mean are they a 'space cadet', likely to blow a gasket at any moment, but are they calm under pressure? Do they take a moment to assess a problem or issue, before making a comment or making a suggestion? You can't put a value on stability in the team and in individuals. It helps build a team that works together better, understands each other and can, to an extent, predict how each other will react to a situation.

If it is an individual, you have to ask, 'Are they in control? Do they know what is going on; not necessarily in immense detail, but enough to make a call if they need to? Do their people know what is expected of them and are they well briefed?'

Does the individual occupy the right shape? A tricky one, but in their team, and in yours are they in the right place, for what they have to offer? Are they respected and given the right status?

In short, the 'head position' equals the person you are coaching. They need to be stable, in the right place in the hierarchy, they need to be respected for their skill, knowledge or experience, or a combination of the three and they need to be able to make a decision and carry the right balance of authority and responsibility to be effective.

This is fundamental to everything that follows. What can happen, if this is wrong, is equivalent to all the potential sporting disasters we looked at earlier.

Lack of consistency will always unsettle the team. A person in the wrong job or at the wrong level will either be bored, under-utilised or be a complete waste of space. Any one of these will have an adverse affect on productivity. So they must be stable and capable in their role. If they don't control what is going on and be on top of the work, people in their teams will take advantage, things will not get done on time or excuses will drift in. The dynamics of the individual and their team also need to be right. If they have a deputy, who they can rely on, or people they can delegate to, then they should take the opportunity to delegate some of their responsibilities to make the team dynamic work better for them. Ultimately they are still accountable, but it puts them in a better coaching position too. They can coach their deputy and develop them to be a reliable and well informed number two.

So if they are lacking in any of these areas, how do you coach them to get them where they should be?

In sport, when someone is learning the right technique, it is often demonstrated to them by someone who can already do it right. So it may be that by using examples of others (not comparisons though), you may be able to show them how to achieve these things. For example, you might say, look at Manager A, he has a team brief every morning for ten minutes to bring everyone up to speed on what's going on. Look at Manager B, he lets each of his team leaders run his weekly meetings in rotation, so they get exposure to the feel of presenting and running a meeting. They are little tips and hints that are designed to help stimulate ideas and methods they might then adopt. Don't tell them that is what they should do; offer them as observations or suggestions.

A fundamental trick in coaching though, which we will discuss later is about how much you coach. A coaching point is not training; it is not counselling; it is not a ticking off. It is primarily and fundamentally constructive. It is a tweak, possibly part of an ultimate objective, which will be achieved by a number of similar tweaks over a period of time. When you hit a Golf ball for the first time, having been shown the technique, chances are it won't fly 250 yards. To achieve that, you may need several different tweaks or coaching points, each one adding yardage. Don't expect to be able to coach someone in a day, to do what it takes years to learn by just practice alone.

My son teaches and coaches Wing Chun. This is a martial art from China and a form of Kung Fu. In their 'coaching' sessions, students are coached through the complex movements and forms, executing them in a very slow and controlled manner. These are done repeatedly at slow speeds until the muscle control and movement is almost programmed in. Then they start adding speed and correction is 'coached' as they inevitably make mistakes.

I can remember my first driving lesson. I recall that the instructor said of the clutch, 'You will have more trouble with that pedal than with any other control.' It was true. To a novice driver, the clutch is a nightmare even when its operation is explained and practice is allowed. It takes practice and time to programme that *feel* into the left leg and foot. And it is programmed in, believe me. If you are in any doubt about that, try braking with your left foot. On second thoughts don't.

Remember this simple phrase; *'Teach in, Coach out.'* When you teach, you are putting something into the individual. This could be a skill, a process, a piece of knowledge. When you coach, you are bringing out of the individual their ability to complete that process, use that skill or acquired knowledge by improving and refining it. This simple principle will be called upon in later chapters and should not be forgotten. If the ability or knowledge is not there to start with, you will not be able to coach it.

There is a principle in one of the most popular games on the planet, which you can use when you are thinking about your team dynamic. It is not a sport, but it is based upon warfare. The game in question is Chess. In Chess, if you are familiar with it, each type of piece moves differently and has unique characteristics, but all of them are working toward the same ultimate goal. If you think of the playing field, or your place of work as the Chessboard and the personalities, skills and talents of the people in your team as the Chess pieces, you will realise that they all do move in different ways and directions, and all have a part to play in helping the team achieve its objective. So don't treat them all the same in terms of how you coach them, position them or attempt to move them. I know we have to accept that legally, you have to treat people equally, but you can still coach people according to who they are and how they might react. I think a good point to make here is that even the lowliest piece in Chess, has a potentially massive part to play. Don't discard or ignore them.

In your coaching, don't be afraid to try out new techniques and methods, use the principle of the leading edge. The *leading edge* is generally defined as the front edge of an Airplane wing, which hits the air first. The leading edge is shaped to force slower air over the top of the wing and faster air underneath, thus creating lift. It is this design that was critical to us learning to craft flying machines and its fundamental message is one of dynamics, direction and pace. In business, if you are at the leading edge you are essentially creating lift; inspiring, trying out new things and changing the accepted dynamics. Give people the opportunity to work with these things, they will be inspired.

Remember to keep the equilibrium in what you do. Without balance, many of the things we have discussed will not work properly. Equilibrium is one of the fundamentals of nature and these should never be ignored. Some Council's in Britain in the 1980's sought to take competitiveness out of the school curriculum. This involved not having examinations or tests, unless they were the official government backed, matriculation board, examinations and no sports day. In my view a criminal act. The idea was all about preventing the less gifted academics or sportspeople, feeling like failures. As a result, a generation of children grew up believing that the business world was a fair, level, playing field with equal opportunities for everyone. Again, you could argue that it is all about balance. Draw a parabolic curve. There will be fewer at the bottom end and fewer at the top end and the rest in the middle, no matter how high you set the bar that will always be the case. You have to accept that and react accordingly. We are naturally and instinctively competitive as a species. It might upset people in some sectors of our society, but it is fact. If we lose sight of that or pretend that it's a bad thing, we will not progress, we will not develop our society or move forward, because there will be no incentive to try. If there is no incentive to improve, there is no place for coaching or coaches.

Whilst the shortest distance between two points is a straight line and you should encourage people to look for the shortest and most direct routes to achieving their goals, be mindful that the straight line is not necessarily always the easiest. Consider the path from one side of a mountain to the other. It might be four miles; two up to the top and two down the other side. The alternative might be a seven mile trip around the mountain, but one which is far easier and requires less technical ability to execute. Coach your people to look at all possible alternatives and not to just plump for the first one or the one which looks the easiest.

As in the water, if you are not in the right position, you will create drag and it will slow you down. You should examine the type of things are creating drag in your team and with individuals. Are they bad at completing processes and general administration, do they need coaching on that? Are they slow in understanding certain aspects of the job, which can cause delays? Is it something external to your team, which you have to coach them to deal with? How can you improve that and eliminate that drag?

1.2. Put the worst thing right first

"We cannot direct the wind, but we can adjust the sail." Unknown.

In sport, when you are coaching an individual or a team you should always look for the worst thing first. Fix that then move to the next worst and so on.

Why the worst thing you may ask? Why not the easiest thing to cure? Go for the quick wins. NO! Categorically NO! Often, the worst thing may be the cause of a number of other problems which you may then need to come up with coaching points for. You will end up correcting every one of them repeatedly. I'll give you an example.

In watching a swimmer executing the front crawl stroke, you notice that their body is prone to zigzag from around the hips. The kick is almost non-existent and the general balance in the water is poor. In short, there is a lot wrong with the stroke. The quick fix, the easy fix is to get them to kick faster and more consistently to add speed, but that won't cure the main fault.

We are actually back to the head again. The head is lifting slightly as they turn to breathe; throwing the body out of line and out of plane in the water, the body flailing from side to side is also happening as a result of this and making it harder to kick as the direction of the body – and therefore the legs - is continually changing. I'd get them to imagine their head is on a kind of axle, right through the centre and in line with the body. It can only turn from side to side. It can't lift, just roll. This will most likely cure the body drift, the leg kick will become easier – although it may need to be quickened up with a later coaching point – and the balance in the water will be addressed at the same time. So, by curing the worst thing, you have rectified several other ills, which you can now fine tune. Got it? Not quite? Let's try another example.

In observing a Golfer, you notice that the ball may always slice out to the right (right handed golfer). You notice that in his stance his feet are not 90 degrees to the target, the shoulders are not level and the golfer is compensating for these two things by turning his head back to 90 degrees from the target, so it is not in the right position relative to his shoulders. As a result, there is a tendency to try and compensate during the swing, to hit the ball cleanly. A person will generally over-compensate and this results in him striking across the ball, right to left, hence the slice to the right. So what do you correct first? His stance; By correcting that, all the other elements he needs to get right, which he has been trying so hard to do correctly, will come naturally.

So, you see from the sporting examples, if you can fix *THE* worst thing, it may often correct a number of other things. Do you think that this applies to people and business coaching?

Well, in my view, of course it does. What takes skill is deciding what the worst thing is. To do this you might list a number of things you want to coach a person on. Let's take a look at a typical list of five things that might occur to you, when you observe and think about that person.

- He's always late for meetings.
- He never seems prepared.
- He often doesn't complete actions given to him.
- He always has to come back to you with an answer to a question.
- He's always whining that he's too busy.

Now, look at that list objectively. The answer should be jumping out at you. What is the worst thing on that list? To my mind, its number two, you may have a different answer, so let me convince you why I think number two is the worst thing. All of the others are about time management or organisation. Preparation is the key to them all. If you prepare for a meeting, you will be on time. You will have the answers to at least some of the questions people may ask. If you plan your time effectively you will complete your actions. If you are too busy it is either that you have too much to do, or you are just not managing your time properly. So, as a coach, tackle that one first. Give him hints and tips on preparation.

In the Military services, you might hear about the seven P's. *Proper planning and preparation, prevents piss-poor performance.* It is a key phrase in ensuring that people prepare and plan. In the Army certainly, and in some sports, this can be a life or death difference.

'Prepare for your day, plan it out. Create a 'to do' list, prioritise. Manage your diary and plan time in to prepare for meetings and complete actions. Make looking at your week the first thing you do on Monday morning, and looking at your day, the first thing you do each morning.' You might suggest that the things to do list is split into, 'must do' tasks and 'would like to do' tasks, so that the priorities are more easily identified. There are a number of coaching points just on that one element, take them one at a time, but make preparation for everything the keynote.

One other important thing to consider, when you are setting out on this analysis, is what is the next worst thing? Now it may be that the first action you take will fix that as well, as we have already seen, but you still need to consider what the next worst, unconnected element is and how you might coach for that. You have to keep the momentum going. - More about that a little later.

In our sport examples, let us consider the swimmer again. We've coached them to set their head in the right position, which has brought them flatter in the water and stopped the destructive lateral movement. Now we need to work on that kick, which has never been right whilst they have been zigzagging. You might use 'tools' to help them practice their kick, such as a kick float, but look closely at the kick. Are they kicking fast enough, with their toes pointed and turned slightly in, so that their foot kicks against the water like a blade? Are their ankles loose to get that extra whip into the last part of the kick? Look for the coaching points and refine that kick.

Now, let us get back to our team member again. He is now managing his time better, preparing his day, prioritising and being more effective. He's even stopped whining, even though he's now completing more work! So what was one of the initial faults that can now be fine tuned, now that he's organising his time? Think about the kick, the consistent propulsion in the swim. What's the propulsive element in that list? In this case, it is the meetings. They are driving most of his work. That's where he picks up the actions, that's where he has to answer questions, that's what he has to make time for and prepare for. So, how do we change his view of the meetings and improve that propulsive element?

Now this next suggestion is a little controversial, but why not let him run the meeting once in a while or even run it completely going forward? Start by letting him run a part of it, a section, then build up to running the whole thing. Sometimes, letting someone try something allows them to view the cause of their former distress from a different angle and grow in the process. In this way they can put it in its place. By organising the meeting, inviting people, setting the agenda and running it, you will see the dawning of realisation as he looks from the opposite side of the fence.

Fundamentally, in your area of work, the most difficult aspect of what we have discussed here is deciding what the key things are and aligning them to the analogy of the position of the head. In an administrative role it may be that there is a strict sequence for the work to be done. It might be that elements of the processes they complete have to align with other elements of the business and that these have a certain criticality or are time-bound. In an engineering or I.T. environment the key elements might be about compatibility of hardware and systems, which comes back to the architectural aspects and planning involved in getting those elements right.

It might sound like a difficult thing to disseminate, but really, if you know your business well, you should be able to pull something together and work from it. Even if you don't get it quite right to start with and need to correct it later, at least you will have made a start and often that is the catalyst which sets you off on the right track.

Be under no illusion, that until coaching in your workplace becomes second nature to you; indeed almost a habit, you will find it is hard work. Coaching is all about thinking and thinking, constantly, is tiring.

You have to feel the effort – There have been many days, where I have sat down after a hard day and reflected that I had really earned my corn that day. The effort expended and the exhaustion as a result of it is tangible. It is when you feel that effort and sometimes even pain, you know that you are performing like an athlete. You can see the agony etched in their faces, when they have really pushed hard to achieve. We can all deliver that kind of effort, if we try.

1.3. Catch Point

"Our reach must exceed our grasp." **Steve Hewitt.**

There is a critical point in swimming, in each competitive stroke called 'catch'. This is the point at which the swimmer feels that they have a weight of water behind their hands ready to pull against. It is an instinctive 'feel' that is usually experienced and then repeated. You feel for the still water at the extension of the stroke then pull through it. It is generally that part of the stroke which determines how effective the rest of it is going to be. In effect when you catch the water and when you release it has a direct correlation to your speed.

At full reach and without dropping your elbow, feel like you are tipping your finger-tips over the front of a barrel (again flexing at the wrist), which will start the catch. At the same time you start bending the elbow and pressing back on the water with the forearm in a near-vertical position.

You should keep your elbows high throughout the stroke, but a memorable way to think about this action whilst you are swimming is to visualise a smiley face drawn on the palm of your hand. As you start the catch, tip your finger tips down and show that smiley face on your palm to the wall you just left. This is like locking your hand in place, effectively feeling-the-water. You will now be pressing the water back behind you rather than pushing it down. Why am I being so technical, you may wonder? This is not going to help *you* in business. Well, it is just to help you think that there are topics that you will coach on which are technical; break them down into components. This will help you and them to understand more about what it is you are doing.

There is also that point in Golf, where contact with the ball is made with the clubs sweet spot, where that impact and the sound it makes tells you that this is going to be a great shot. I daresay, that when a top footballer makes contact with the ball from a free kick and curls it sweetly into the top corner, that there is a moment as he makes contact, when he knows he's hit it well.

Catch in swimming is something that comes with practice. Knowing about it and being coached in it is a very small element in the process. It is something you have to experience and programme in, like the Wing Chun moves I mentioned earlier.

So what is the business coaching equivalent of catch? In Swimming it is that feeling that the effort you put in is being converted into motion more effectively and in some cases with less effort. It is a feeling of engagement with the media you are in. You are 'in the zone' as they say. In business it is about traction. When you are well prepared, have anticipated the answers, know your subject really well and have a positive meeting or draft a really great email, it is the equivalent of that catch point. You know it is the trigger that sets everything off in the right direction, at the right speed. So, is catch something tangible, which we can coach? Remember, we are *coaching out*, we're not *teaching in*. A good coaching point in this context would be to coach your people and teams to look for the key elements that will add traction to a piece of work. Traction is not "Because the CEO wants it doing." That is more of a motivating or equally a de-motivating factor. Traction is about generating enthusiasm, a head of steam, a 'can do, let's do', attitude. So in terms of looking for the trigger point it is about engagement. It is about finding that one thing or several things that will fire a person's enthusiasm and imagination. Never say things like, "The boss wants it done, so just do it." People will resent that and believe that they could be doing something more worthwhile or productive. Look for those positive triggers, "This is going to save thousands of pounds a year," or "This is groundbreaking stuff." People like to be doing work which is interesting, adds value and can be appreciated. They like to do work they can be proud of and talk about. Look for those triggers to 'catch' that will present them with those things.

If you've ever played Golf, in every round, no matter how bad the Scorecard looks, there will always have been that one shot, that perfect combination of rhythm, timing, control and execution that puts a smile on your face. Catch in this context is about all those elements coming together as the club makes contact with the ball and the follow through is executed. Wouldn't it be good to feel like that after every shot? Translating that in business terms, it is catch or engagement that is responsible for that feeling of satisfaction, knowing that you have done a good job. Again, wouldn't it be good to feel like that after every piece of work? Make sure, as part of your coaching, that you identify to people what that point is, and how important it is to engage properly with the work, the people and other resources involved in it.

Let's not make any secret of the fact though that, like a good swim, or a great round of golf, you may feel physically drained at the end of it. Work is about putting in the effort to achieve. Coaching is making sure that none of that effort is wasted and that we actually grow and develop as a consequence. When you feel the traction, when things start to move, that is not the time to slacken off, that is precisely the time to put the hammer down. In the next section we will discuss that concept further, but you must recognise that this sort of approach is not meant to get easier with familiarity. All that happens is that the focus, intensity and sometimes the pace changes up a gear. Coaching just equips you to handle it. You don't believe me? Think of an Olympic Athlete, training, being coached, physically developed to the peak of their performance, does their sport get easier? Does attending and competing in the world's largest event, with their peers, who have been equally honed to perfection make it easier? Not for an instant. The fact that they are there, have qualified and are able to compete means that they have been coached to cope with the pressure.

We have discussed traction and hitting that point at which things start to move in the right direction and at the right pace. It is a great feeling to know that what you are working on is alive and has a head of steam. Just as it is exciting to see one of the people you coach in sport accelerate away from the rest, or score a goal, or hit a shot pin high and have a tap in. You can see, feel and experience, that momentum which you have helped initiate actually achieving something. Traction is a wonderful thing.

Having achieved it, you must endeavour to maintain it and that means looking for those elements that might cause it to fail.

In swimming, the next stroke has to be as good as the one you have just completed, and the next and the next. In business terms, that means consistency in the way you work. If you are a coach you have to inspire and enliven your team so that they feel enthusiastic, even excited about making that next piece of work or element just as effective as the previous one, no matter how mundane or ordinary it might seem. In a record breaking or Gold medal winning swim, you could look at every single stroke the swimmer has made in detail and would probably see that they were all executed to a similar standard. It is not just the last few that won the race. It was all those others, perfectly executed and solidly performed. This is quite a strong principle to try to get across in business and one to look out for. There are parts of all our work that we either dislike doing or feel that it is a necessary evil; report writing, filling in forms and that type of thing. Generally, people will deal with these in a lack-lustre way and not really take a great deal of care with them. They will just dash them off as quickly as possible and move on to the next, more exciting thing.

If you want people to lose traction and waste that 'catch' momentum in their work and career, allow them to treat elements of it like that. Lack of effort or diligence in one area could and will spill over into other areas. You must Coach excellence in all the little tasks and sundry jobs. They are attention to detail and help maintain shape and discipline.

1.4. Dynamics

So far, with our swimmers, we've made them adopt the right shape in the water, we've identified some key coaching points to help speed them along and we've talked about catch, that initial point at which everything is poised and ready to deliver a great stroke. There is an obvious problem with that. As with Golf, one really great focussed and powerful stroke does not make a winning swim or round. In Swimming, from the point of catch onwards, there are adjustments and a lot of thinking to be done, throughout the stroke, to ensure that the initial catch and pull are not wasted; like golf, swimming is a thinkers sport.

Water is an unusual medium. In no other sport do you engage with the medium so closely – although Skiing comes close - and, as we know, water moves about. At the point of catch, there is a mass of still water awaiting the start of your pull, but once you apply force to it, it starts to move with you. If you keep your hand moving either in the same direction or at the same speed, you will quickly lose the traction you began with. So the coaching lesson here would be to think about the nature of the medium you are in, and to change the direction of your hand to catch as much still water as possible and/or accelerate the hand through the pull, so that if it starts moving, you are still moving faster than it, and therefore continue to be able to push against it. A Front crawlers hand will extend out forwards in front of them, turn slightly out to catch, the elbow will then bend as the hand travels inwards and close under the body, down the centre line and out from the waist pushing out to full extension at the side. It is in this last section that the hand should be travelling at its fastest. Knowing the medium you are dealing with is important to this process. Knowing the nature of water will explain why you need to accelerate your pull. Know your business and where you need to make changes in pace.

In Golf too, if the rhythm of the swing is right, the club head will always be chasing the hands and body through the swing, so that the flex in the

wrists and the natural flex of the club shaft make that last section of the swing, from the hands passing the centre, to contact, the fastest section of its journey, as it whips through, striking the ball.
As you might have guessed, this type of dynamics can be applied to coaching in the workplace. Again, we need to consider what the sporting examples are telling us about their particular dynamics.

We've talked about how 'catch' or engagement in a piece of work can effectively kick start a process. Whether that process is a simple piece of work or a project, the right start, gaining traction and gathering momentum, is important to the initiation. Now it's moving and people are fired up and enthused. Think about the medium you are in. This could be the fast moving consumer goods industry, government, engineering, whatever it might be the medium will have its own dynamic. It will move in a particular way and at a particular pace. There may need to be several changes in pace and direction to maintain the overall pace of the job.

It is important to know and be able to anticipate this movement and potential changes in direction, and be able to stay at the head of it, driving it. If you let any aspect of that job get ahead of you or you lose your engagement with it, your control is gone and there will be a lot of wasted effort expended.

In swimming, the way you do that is through direct feedback. You can feel tiny changes in the water and your interaction with it. You constantly think and adjust your hand position and speed of pull to maintain that advantage. In our business context, you need to do exactly the same. Don't wait for the feedback, ask for it, chase it down and use it. People in unchallenging environments tend to wait for the next project or progress meeting to assemble the feedback. By then, it is too late. Imagine the same scenario in the Swimming.
"How did I do?"
"You lost."
"Why?"

"You needed to speed up your hands through the pull, but you didn't." Too late; if you wait for the next meeting or update, you are already behind, have lost momentum and control. So, in the coaching highlight the value of putting something in your daily 'must do' list, about catching up with certain key pieces of work. Make a few *drive by's* to peoples offices and desks and just throw in a cursory, *'Is everything okay with the project?'* or *'Have you completed that action?'* By doing so, you will be in a better position to make decisions about which direction to pull and what speed to pull at. Does something need more emphasis? Do you need to approach someone or something differently? Don't be afraid of altering the dynamic. That is why it is called a dynamic.

Now let us consider two aspects of this in relation to the swimming example and in doing so try to avoid a common mistake people make in their work. In swimming we have already said that it is fundamental to search for the still water. Find that, instinctively or by changing the direction of the hands and the greater the impact in increasing your speed and the efficiency of your stroke.

In the process of executing their work what people tend to do is to continue to pull at the areas already moving, in other words, where their efforts are easier to expend, but less likely to be rewarded. The trick here is to search for the 'still water'. What is it in this piece of work or project that's not moving? What is it that doesn't seem to have been disturbed by the stroke or the catch? Focus on that and get your hand in there! You may find that, as a result there are unexpected gains. If you are trying to encourage an employee to do the same, you may discover that he has been staying in his comfort zone, or an area of expertise with which he is particularly conversant. It may be that the areas he has left alone are managed by someone he is afraid to tackle. This will need addressing. Whatever the reason, it is important to think about maintaining that initial momentum you have gained and always looking for ways to sustain it. There is no such thing as a lull in a competitive swim, equally there is no such thing as a lull in a project or a piece of work. Keep on it and stay focussed on the job as a whole.

I was involved in a project a few years ago where there was a relatively short window to achieve a large number of similar tasks. They were effectively technical conversions of a business acquisition. There were thirty three to do in twelve weeks and the lead time, from inception to the first few going live was just under seven weeks. For three of those weeks, communications were sparse and the momentum certainly had not built. We relied upon the feed from other areas for our data, to allow us to plan what we had to do. I had to take the decision to get the ball rolling, for our area of the project; otherwise we would have run out of time. In the absence of any decisions, direction or even a steer, I put our programme together and called our team in to brief them on what would be required. There were tasks they needed to do now, in advance of the main programme, so we started them off with those and awaited the main head of steam. It was slow in coming, but it gave our team some focus and they were ready to scale up the operation once it all kicked off.

When the programme did arrive, the goalposts had been moved slightly and instead of a three week rolling programme covering twelve weeks, we were now looking a two week rolling programme covering eight weeks. This meant that our carefully engineered plan for each location had to be shortened by a third. There were some standard tasks and dependencies, built in, which could not be changed, we just had to re-engineer that three week process and ensure that the end result was the same. Whilst it sounds easy, you are not actually changing the time it takes to execute some tasks. They can't physically be done any faster. What you may have to do is operate some in parallel, or overlap others. It's a bit like moving from competitive swimming to water polo. I've still got to be able to swim fast, but now there's a ball in here with me and a goal to aim at. So you have a whole new set of things to be aware of, engage with and maintain focus on. In these situations, you must be on the top of your game all the time and be constantly reviewing and changing your own dynamic. If one programme slips, all the subsequent ones are affected.

There is one other thing to think about in terms of the dynamics of the medium you are working in. Again, we must first go back to the water. I say water rather than pool, because people don't just swim in pools, they also swim in open water; in lakes, rivers and seas. There is one thing that water does which we have already discussed. Once it is disturbed, it moves. The sea has waves, rivers have a natural flow or current and even lakes are affected by movement. Believe it or not, so are pools. That is why the fastest qualifiers are assigned to the centre lanes, they have earned an advantage. In the centre of the pool, the disturbance of the water is less than it is near the walls. If you think about it, you have eight powerful swimmers striking out in the same direction. As they pass through the water their 'wash' is left behind them and forms a triangle, like at the stern of a boat. This widens, as the swimmer gets further away, until it hits the wall, then it starts to come back across the pool again. I think we all understand currents and waves in open water. The point is, that there are other things going on in that medium, other than your own efforts, which will directly affect your performance. There are few other non contact sports where the medium or the efforts of others has an impact on you so directly, that's why swimming is a good example to use in relation to work.

So what are the currents and waves we have to be aware of in work? Equally, what can we do about them? Primarily, knowing that they are there is a good start. It is to an extent the political aspects of doing a job. A strong current or wave may knock you off course in a swim. In your work, it could be resistance to change, someone who doesn't see eye to eye with you, or even someone who criticises what you are doing behind your back. How do we combat the strong currents and waves in a swim? We are aware of them; we feel for them and watch for them. We can, if we time it right, even use them. In work it is just the same. Be absolutely aware of the currents and waves and any 'wash' bouncing off the walls.

This might sound glib and as if I am trivialising it, but it is not that easy. You really have to make a conscious effort to do it. As a coaching point, it is all about communication.

In any piece of work, or project, you will have stakeholders. People who the work is being done for, on behalf of or who are budget holders. There will also be those who are not affected directly by the work, but may be secondarily affected. Finally, there may be people not affected directly, but who simply don't agree with it. These groups or individuals are where the currents and waves can come from. Some of the waves will be massive breakers, which you should be able to see coming and hopefully ride, but there will be others which are under-currents, silent and almost invisible. This is where good communication comes in. You have to coach to make sure that the individual not only communicates to the stakeholders effectively, but ensures that they get feedback coming through from lots of sources. This could be formal communication, or just ground whispers that they pick up. If there are any of the latter, they should not be ignored. For example if a person working on a project hears a whisper that one of the stakeholders is not happy about a particular contractor, there needs to be an open question asked. It might be as simple as, 'I've heard that there are some concerns about.....' and let them do the rest. Remember it is people you are dealing with and the more open, honest and transparent you are, the more likely you are to be able to deal with waves and currents.

1.5. The next worst thing

"The smaller the detail the greater the value." Doug Johnson.

We've already looked at dealing with the worst thing first and how that may help solve a number of other issues. In that discussion we touched upon looking for the next worst thing. Not only that, but being aware of the next worst thing at the point of coaching on the previous point, to keep the momentum going.

There has to be that kind of order to it, not just because by fixing the worst thing you may cure several other things in the process, but because these are the real quick wins. Fixing something immediately, because it looks easy, may not be such a good idea longer term. You may end up having to change that very same thing again later, several times, as you work through the coaching plan. If you plan your coaching points in a structured way, you can always drop some of them if by changing one thing, one larger thing, you cure others. Sports coaches start by knowing what the ultimate goals are. There are very definite targets in coaching individuals and teams. You want to achieve a better time, distance, score more goals or just deliver a better performance than the opponent. However, to take one of the examples, it is no good scoring five goals every match, if your team frequently concedes six or more. There may be several steps to take in turning around the fortunes of a team like that, but the first one would probably not be to start scoring more goals.

There has to be a structure to what you do and the way you tackle it and it is not just an intuitive thing; it is strategic. You can still have the ultimate goal in mind, it is a necessity, but you plan the strategic milestones and the journey to achieving them by looking at all the elements you are going to have to address to get there. You might draw a diagram. Listing down all the things that need to be corrected then mark out the primaries. Identify the worst thing and what that will resolve, then the next worst and what that will resolve and so on. There may be several stages to what you have to do, but it will be mapped out and have a structure you can use, follow and, if appropriate, share.

Largely, it all depends on your ultimate aims. Think back to our earlier sporting examples. Let's take Golf again this time. You've managed to get your man hitting straight and a reasonable distance. You might be happy at that point, knowing that, with further coaching points, he is going to achieve enough distance to get to the green in one, two, or three shots, depending on whether it's a par 3, 4 or 5 hole. So we can be fairly confident that he will achieve 80% of his objective, using the 80/20 rule – more about that later. You might now like to think about his putting. A lot of the skill in putting is not so much about the control of the club and the speed and distance factors, but about reading the greens. He may be striking the ball just right, managing to get the ball 'pin high', but the ball is veering away, when he putts, because he's not reading the green properly. So imagine what you might do to help him overcome that particular issue.

If you're not a golfer, don't worry. I am about to explain. What you do as a coach is to get the player to look at the position of the ball and the ideal line he should try to follow to the hole. Now, the ideal line may have a few things to take into consideration. It might not just be a flat straight run. It may have a slope to the left or right away from the ideal line, or even both, at different points. What your man needs to do is to look at that line from a number of different angles and see what the best approach should be. For example, it might be that his initial stroke should head right of the hole, because the lie of the land will bring it back left.

In our world of work, we could probably translate that quite easily and directly into looking at the job in hand, from a number of angles. To achieve A, B and C, you may have to go via D and E first. You may have to take into consideration the lie of the land. Don't just assume that you can take a task and initiate it simply and without any possible deflections. I have heard and witnessed a number of such assumptions and their consequent outcomes. There is the old adage that to assume, is to make an Ass out of U and Me; quite appropriate. So there are a number of coaching points regarding the path a piece of work or a task might take and it is all about the terrain, the amount of change and who or what that might have an impact on, and not just *assuming* that the straight, most obvious and most direct path will be the one least fraught with difficulty. The main coaching points then could be, never assume anything and always assess the impact of change at each stage. As far as the terrain goes, this could be the infrastructure or the department affected by the task. Are there any likely obstacles or bumps that might affect the smooth implementation of the work? Look at it from their point of view, go around the other side of the target and look back, like a golfer would with the shot they were planning; that is the key. Don't just walk up and whack the ball in the general direction of the hole, that's what you do off the tee, not on the green. As you implement change, as you take those crucial shots that require more accuracy and touch, you need to plan them. Just so, in the execution of a task you need to plan your move, plan changes and be sure to take full account of the terrain. A golfer will do all of that and then, in his head, imagine the outcome. He will imagine stroking the ball with a particular amount of pace and visualise its path to toward the hole. That is what you must coach people to do. Plan, visualise, adjust, execute. How is it going to play out? How is it going to look? What twists and turns are going to be taken? Is this shot just going to get me close enough to finish off, or will I need that second putt?

In Golf, a professionals average round (PAR) is based upon 1,2 or 3 shots and two putts, depending on the length of the hole from tee to flag. It is therefore expected that, most of the time, even a professional will require two putts. One shot to get close, one to drop the ball in the cup. In a task, you could really take the same view. That first putt, which we have just discussed, is the hardest one. It is going to get you close enough for a tap in. In the task, or project, it is the one which is going to close off most of the final 20% of the whole thing. The tee shot and the chip have been the 80%. In a task or project that last 20% will take you 80% of the time. It is the detail, the precision the finishing touches that make a good job great. How many times have you seen a Golfer hit the green on schedule and three putt? It is usually that first one that does all the damage. If he doesn't take his time, assess it from a variety of angles and most importantly, make sure that he is mentally ready to take it he will fail. This is a phenomenon that you can see all the time in sport, not just in golf either. Any sport where you get one chance to execute the task and one chance to get everything right, demonstrates this perfectly. Sometimes, even watching these events unfold, you can tell whether the sportsman is ready or not. It's about their preparatory routines, body language and facial expressions. It is also crucially about how important that moment might be. Consider some of these situations in sport; A penalty kick in a cup final or qualifier, a Putt (as we've already discussed) to win the Open, a high dive with a complicated series of moments within it, a high jump. These are just some of the sports where no matter how experienced, professional, well practiced or skilled the exponent, they can still get it wrong if they try to execute it before they are actually, mentally ready.

What then do we do to ensure that our man is mentally ready? How do we coach him to make sure that he makes his moves at the right moments? Clearly some of it is about learning from experience, but there is one key factor to consider. That factor is doubt. If you have any doubts before you try to execute any of these things, including, in a task, that crucial e-mail, an instruction, go-ahead or decision. Stop! Take a step back, look at it again. Am I sure that's how the land lies; am I sure that's the right angle of take off; am I sure I'm going to put this to the keepers left? In business; have I communicated clearly enough; does everyone know what they are doing; is everyone onside with the decision; have I missed anything? Doubt usually infers that there is something that hasn't been fully explored or confirmed, that there are still unanswered questions.

We started off in this section looking for the next worst thing and the example we have given is about detail, engagement and communication. It is all relevant. It is all pertinent to our overall discussion. There are many things that we may identify as coaching points, but the rule still applies; deal with the worst thing first, then the next, then the next. What you will find is that, as you progress, the items and coaching points are more detailed and need more analysis. This is to be expected. Fine tuning of any kind is just that, it is at much more of a macro level and tiny adjustments make a big difference. By dealing with the worst thing first you have probably dealt with a large proportion of what needs attention, i.e. the more obvious and visible elements; but the detail needs more time, more work and ultimately more finesse.

Generally, managers will spend their time and energies focusing on the 'hard' topics. Processes, resources, control and planning; all the things you can teach in from a manual. They neglect the softer skills, the people aspects because they require you to fundamentally change the way you work. Many of the greatest world class leaders are not simply good process managers, they don't have to be. The processes are there to be followed and conformed to. Instead they are brilliant coaches. The coaching they impart is constructive and developmental and it is executed on a continual basis.

You cannot leave coaching to a quarterly or annual review. Neither should you make coaching a weekly spot in the diary. There should be a cadence to it, which you establish; Target – Coach – Practice – Review - Analyse. Small, seemingly insignificant tweaks are the fastest way to achieve changes in behaviour and the culture. If you try to impose large changes, you will probably go backwards. Think about the sporting examples again. Would you give a Golfer a brand new set of Clubs, on the day of an important tournament? Would you invite a Swimmer to change their stroke technique, just before a race? No, of course you wouldn't, you would gradually introduce change, over a period of time so that output wasn't affected, but ultimately there was an improvement in the whole level.

You cannot coach by trying to implement huge rafts of improvement or by trying to change the manner in which coaching is done. It is largely about the mindset you adopt and the way you approach the whole culture that invites the people you are coaching to change it. You cannot achieve this unless you believe in what you are doing and essentially live and breathe it. If you believe that coaching works and that your take on it will produce results, it will. You can't expect your team to believe unless it is obvious that you do. You also have to clear the ground for it to happen. As Brian Souza, author of *The Weekly Coaching Conversation* put it, *'You have to pull weeds, before you can plant seeds.'* I think that describes that initial process perfectly.

To coach effectively you also have to believe that you can take someone with inherent talent and develop them; that they will not just blossom naturally without any coaching. If any other option were true, why would we bother to coach? The cream doesn't actually always rise to the top, sometimes it gets mixed up and fails to separate or it curdles. In our world, this is where you either lose sight of those with the talent, or you disenfranchise or disgruntle them and they lose momentum.

How many bad managers does it take to ruin a potential star's career? Only one, but he doesn't have to do anything to achieve it.

As a manager/coach, what you reinforce are the things that will get done. Where you apply focus, they will apply focus. So if you target their work or opportunities to develop which have the wrong impetus or direction, they will get the job done, but nothing else will happen. You have to think about the answer or outcome you want, before you set the goal or ask the question. If a football coach said to a defender, that he wanted him to man-mark a striker from the opposing team and stick to him like glue; that is an instruction, to which the response will be obvious. The defender will try to stick to that player all game, getting drawn out of position, probably outpaced on occasion and not making any other significant contribution. If however the coaching point is, 'don't let him get behind the defensive line, that's where he does the damage.' The player can relax and watch the striker, playing his own game but make sure he doesn't get into those danger zones. If you coach randomly, sporadically or without the correct focus, you will not realise the true benefits.

Once again, if you think about swimming, a swimmer may start off being able to swim 100 metres front crawl in 1 minute 30 seconds. Knowing that the world's best are cracking the 50 second mark, with the right adjustments and application of basic principles, you could probably coach a good swimmer of between 14-16 yrs old down to 65 seconds in a reasonable time period, even in under a year. That last ten seconds however, is going to take a lot longer. It is about the detail, those fine adjustments that deliver the finesse and the medals.

In creating the overall structure you can't and shouldn't try to separate coaching from the actual operation you are coaching in. Whether it is in sport or in business, the main activity must occupy the same space as the coaching and it must be clear that it is integral to the end result. It is not a separate entity, bolted on. Many of the key parts of our daily operation in business are related to coaching and we should embrace that, rather than feeling we are shoe-horning a coaching session in to cope with it.

Take, for example, five of the main operational functions we may encounter any day of the week these are; Change, Team Building, Performance management; Strategy and Facilitation. If we look at sports coaching, it is clearly be involved in all these areas as a matter of course. This should also be true in business. Generally it isn't because we don't position the coaching correctly in our working structures.

If you don't believe me on this point, then answer these simple questions. If we make changes, to infrastructure, dynamics, our overall goals; do we coach what that means to our teams? If we look at performance statistics, do we just simply groan at them and ask people what they are doing about it, or do we break it down, analyse it, come up with coaching points and feed them back to the team? When the business strategy is revealed, do we analyse it and align our coaching to the strategy. Or just tell people what it is and expect them to figure that out for themselves? I would suspect that, unless your organisation is mature and has already embraced these principles that you cannot give the right answers to those questions. There are so many opportunities to use coaching in a positive and constructive way and we generally ignore them in business, because we haven't quite figured out how.

In reality, it is not that difficult. We only have to look at the example sport gives us to see where coaching is positioned. In sport, the coach is instrumental in making sure that any changes, either in the laws or rules of the sport are correctly assimilated and any changes to the dynamic of the team are also smoothly transitioned. In fact, change can play a part from game to game; from opponent to opponent. Team building is quite an obvious one, but where the coach deals with an individual sportsperson, that team will actually be the support team, the back room staff. The coach, being the primary interface, will ensure that the team gels together to produce a winning combination. Performance management is where they will look at the performance or match statistics, analyse them and present the revised plan or any coaching points back to the team. Again, strategic aims or goals are fundamental to a sports coaches planning and developmental targets. Facilitation is a slightly harder one, but again, not rocket science. It is about enabling and the provision of the right opportunities.

If you begin to think about a typical day, week or month in your working cycle, break it down and look at what it comprises. Then look at how a sports coach would work in their typical cycle and apply the same principles to it. Instead of the day being mapped out in terms of work or tasks that need to be done, look at what goals can be achieved and what you need to do as a coach to help achieve them. Put time aside for review and analysis and remember, coaching is not training or teaching; it is nurture. If something doesn't work, you change it; you try something else. If you can structure the way you work to build in a regime of coaching, with the coaching cycle firmly embedded, you will start to see goal setting, objectives and targets in a whole new way.

To summarise, in this chapter we have looked at getting the head right, either its position, or the part of the dynamic it is contained in, and then the shape and dynamic of the team or the individual and why that is important. We have looked at the catch point, at what that is and what it means. This is the part at which we engage with the work or project and how to coach our people to do that successfully. One important area we touched upon was doing the less important elements of the work, or the ones where they feel less comfortable, equally as well as those they enjoy. If, as a coach, you can crack that particular nut, you are doing well. We have looked at dealing with coaching in an ordered way, using a structure and looking at the worst thing first, but all the time keeping the goal in mind. In the next chapter we will look at taking that raw shape we have created and turning into a sculpture.

CHAPTER 2.
FROM SHAPE TO SCULPTURE

In this second chapter we will look at refining what we have begun to shape so that it is instantly more recognisable. That could be in terms of the team or an individual. Let's take a swimmer who comes to you for coaching. They swim, perhaps three of the four competitive strokes. Usually Butterfly is the one they can't yet master. Of the ones they can do, they are far from what you would ever hope to call competitive. In order to be recognised as a competitive swimmer, you may have to retrain them in the correct technique for each stroke, add 'Fly' to their repertoire and coach them to become efficient, then fast. If someone comes in flailing arms and legs and using masses of energy in the process, you could leave them to work at that speed, but they actually wouldn't get that much faster. They would create more turbulence and reduce their own traction in the water. The key, then, is to gradually refine that technique and style, then gradually add back in the speed, once they have become effective.

The concept is just the same in business. A whirlwind of a character, possibly a little hyperactive, will not have much finesse or style and will almost certainly create more turbulence than is desirable. You cannot change cultures of work or the approach people have to it, by adding one element that is either opposed to it or otherwise in conflict with it, so why try to disturb the dynamics? Instead, coach what you have to coach first; to be better at what they do, then add speed and efficiency.

In the following pages, we will explore how we approach that and how we turn a roughly hewn block, into something more recognisable and attractive.

2.1. Small achievable corrections

I have already talked about the concept of putting the worst thing right, then the next worst and so on. Generally, after a few cycles of that approach, you will find that you are getting into more detail or finesse. Again the often abused phrase "It's the 80/20 rule," comes into play. The big things that are wrong are corrected with the least amount of time and effort. The final 20% will always take the most effort and time, because it is fine tuning and attention to detail.

Like the swimmer we discussed, correcting the head position cured quite a number of ills, and following on from that there may be many small corrections on elements of the stroke. There would be emphasis on catch, on the acceleration of the pull and maintaining either a balancing or propulsive kick. Closer detail may also be explored, tiny corrections in the position of the hands and feet and how far the head rotates on breathing.

In Golf the corrections may be around the back-swing and adding power and on the follow through, such as the final position of the club. There may be minute corrections on the position of the feet and the distance between the golfer and the ball on the tee.

Each of these corrections, in either sport will be done in a carefully thought out sequence and with an overall aim in mind. It may be increasing speed or distance, accuracy or efficiency. Each will be introduced and practiced and embedded into the routine, before the next is added, the consideration being that you don't want to destroy work you have already done by introducing something else too quickly or which may cause other knock on effects.

In our business example, this principle holds good. You cannot give a person a number of coaching points all at once and expect them to assimilate them. There are a number of reasons for this. Firstly, they may need to be introduced in a strict sequence. We have already said why that is important in our sport examples. Given several points to address, a person may implement them in their own sequence, perhaps starting with the one they consider to be easiest or have a personal preference for. This good work could then be undone by the next one they choose. Secondly, it is not good practice to bombard someone with coaching points. You must therefore, consider the sequence in which coaching points should be applied. Coaching is about a journey, think of the word *coaxing*, it implies a gradual and persuasive approach. You are almost spoon feeding someone to achieve. Thirdly, think about subtlety. A person being coached should not feel like they are a long way adrift from doing a good job. Giving them even two or three points at once could make them feel like they have a long way to go. Finally; and perhaps most obviously, give them too much to think about and they will forget something. Coaching in small, easy to digest, chunks, is also about establishing the patterns and routines you want to build upon.

I have titled this chapter deliberately, From Shape to Sculpture, because it is what we need to do. We need to engineer the basic shape we want and then refine it, gradually applying more and more detail. It is that chipping away which makes the sculpture become recognisable and a work of art. The chipping away which a sculptor does, is not done focussing on just one area, until it is complete. They are constantly reviewing and refining the whole shape, so that it all develops together. If they focussed just on one area, before moving on, it may be that proportions may be lost or affected.

Let's take a look at our colleague again. Earlier we suggested that he ran a meeting or part of a meeting to improve his own preparation skills and perhaps to understand how when managing a meeting, how important it is that those attending have prepared.

Rather than just springing it on him one afternoon, ten minutes before the meeting, you would be better discussing it with him, before the meeting prior to the one you want him to organise. This will allow him to take on board that he will be running the meeting next time and will encourage him to look for key things that he must bring to the organisation. Don't go overboard here. It may just be that you give him these key pointers:

- We have the project meeting later this week.
- I want you to run the next one.
- Take note of the format.
- Note what went well.
- Note what didn't go well.
- Incorporate these findings and thoughts into your meeting.

Now you might think; that's a lot of coaching points. No it isn't. It is one coaching point. The suggestions above are part of the same thing. The coaching point is 'Look at the next meeting with a different pair of eyes, take notes so you can plan how you will run it.' It is then up to him how he deals with that. Much in the same way you might ask a Swimmer or Golfer to incorporate something into their stroke or swing, you might ask them to watch someone else first, but with particular elements to observe more closely. Then they try it for themselves, interpreting what they have seen into their own action. The follow up is just as important. Discussing what they found or how they felt about it. Did they achieve their objective? What would they do differently next time and so on?

One of the key points around this element should also be taken on board. The correction or coaching point should be achievable. That means it should be realistic and a step change rather than a massive one. You would not expect a rookie Golfer with a 28 handicap to suddenly knock 20 strokes off in a single round. It wouldn't happen. You should guard against setting someone up for failure. A failure can set someone back a long way because it is demoralising and also undermines any coaching you have done to date with that individual. Having failed, they will question what they have been told or coached into doing and it may take twice as long to get them back to the point you were at before the failure. No matter how Gung Ho or enthusiastic the person is, you should make the steps realistic.

2.2. Measurable achievements

In our sports, Swimming and Golf, improvement can be measured quite simply by the time achieved or the Scorecard respectively. Are they faster than they were a month ago? Has their average round come down? Or even simpler, are they hitting the green in one, two or three shots, depending on the PAR for that hole.

It is much more difficult when coaching in the workplace to have outcomes which are as specific and measurable as those, particularly if you are talking about a management role, rather than someone completing multiple or repeated processes. You must find a way of measuring the effectiveness of the coaching points if at all possible. Demonstrating to the person receiving the coaching that there has been an improvement is a great motivator and also gives them confidence that the coaching works. They are therefore more likely to listen and try any further suggestions.

As we discussed earlier, you may have a team member who never seems to have any time or complains that they have too much to do. It would be easy in this case to measure the improvement, as they have started to complete additional tasks and organise their time more efficiently. In some other cases it isn't always that simple and we must look for other ways of demonstrating improvement.

It may be worth considering the approach to objectives which is classified by the term SMART – i.e. Specific, Measurable, Achievable, Realistic and Time bound. The actual coaching point does not have to be SMART in that context, but the outcome should be. If we can come up with coaching points which comply with those criteria, perhaps they will be measurable and therefore more likely to have an impact. Whatever criteria you use to measure progress or achievement, and whatever the outcome, you should always be positive. Even if the point made is that, 'What we have learned from that is that it doesn't work in our environment.'

Consider the Swimmer again. The coaching point might be to bring the arm closer to the body through the pull. What is the likely outcome? It might not be a quicker length or distance. It might be that it actually takes fewer strokes to complete the distance, which means a saving in energy. Ultimately, with a few more coaching points that might result in a faster time, but for now, we're after the efficiency.

With our team member, one of his initial faults we observed was that he rarely completed actions assigned to him in meetings. If that had been his only fault, we may have asked him to identify why he wasn't completing them all. We may have discovered that one of the reasons he didn't complete them was that he didn't start thinking about them until a few days before the meeting. A coaching point here might have been to always commence progress on your actions the day after the meeting. This would give him more time for follow up and any relevant chasing. You could then follow that coaching point up by asking for a progress report after three days.

These are things you learn over time, but if they are coached out you can be much more effective, much faster. In a rather large business project a few years ago, I was required to attend a Project Meeting every Tuesday in London. This involved flying into Heathrow for around 8:40 a.m. and being picked up and whisked to the Project Meeting which started at 09:00. The meetings involved many different business areas and could go on for over three hours. As I wasn't booked on the return flight until 15:45, I would immediately start on my actions, making a few calls and firing off emails to those who could get me the answers or a get a piece of work done. By the time I boarded the plane, I generally had answers to 50% of the questions raised or work requests booked in to be done. It is not about being sickeningly efficient or hyperactive. It is about prioritisation and planning. I used my time to best effect. I used the tools I had at my disposal and the resources I could call upon. There is another added benefit to being in the position of closing off all your actions promptly. You get ahead of the game. Instead of waiting to be ambushed at the next meeting with another raft of actions, you can start to be proactive and seek them out. How? We mentioned it in this context earlier. Where was most of the team member's work coming from? Answer, the meeting. Now we drill down. Who in that meeting; which stakeholder/s were the ones raising the bulk of the issues? Once you identify that, you can start to tackle them early. This is what I began to do. I'd set people working on my actions, then a few days before the next meeting I'd get in touch with the key stakeholders and see if they had any new issues and I'd try my best to resolve *those* before the next meeting. Result, fewer and fewer actions came out at the meeting and any whispers of issues were quickly quashed. The outcome was also measurable, in the sense of there being fewer actions. It is not a difficult thing to coach in someone. Don't procrastinate.

Here is another example. There was a piece of widely deployed kit that was perceived to be failing to do its job. I and one of my team were convinced that it wasn't the piece of kit, but the process on how it was used. We had to prove it, so that those responsible would reiterate the process to those using it. They were reluctant to do so, due to the time, costs and logistics involved. I asked one of my Service suppliers to think about what would prove it to him, in his position. He thought about it for a while and then came back with the answer that if it worked effectively at one location, it should work at all locations. Good boy! He went to one of the worst performing locations and asked them what they thought the process was. Their answer was incorrect. He told them what the process should be and stayed with them for half a day to ensure they had taken it on board. When we analysed the data the following day, it was clear that this had worked. There was a 100% return, instead of the unacceptable 93% they had been returning. Without saying anything of our success, we then suggested to those responsible that they took a few locations where the returns were low and asked them to outline what they thought the process was and then if necessary re-iterate the process, just to see what impact that would have. Reluctantly they agreed and saw the same result we had achieved. The point is that you sometimes have to put aside your own convictions and ask yourself, if I was in their position what would swing it for me?

You can be right. You can be right in your own perception, but others may need more convincing. For their own reasons they may need to have conclusive proof. Be prepared to engineer your own work and the coaching of your team to achieve this.

You should never make the assumption that apparent reluctance of a coachee to take on board coaching hints and tips is anything to do with their resistance, or any defensiveness. If you set goals, targets or objectives which are unrealistic or appear to be out of reach, you will trigger that sort of response and you should be able to recognise it. One of the keys to resolving this, or even making sure it doesn't occur in the first place, is to take time to evaluate your own performance. Ask yourself if you have been objective and realistic. Have you been guilty of not practicing what you preach?

I worked under a manager some years ago, who would stack all the negatives up, over the year, until appraisal time. As such, it gave him a huge stick to beat me with, once a year, a plausible excuse for not giving me a merit pay increase and some content, albeit dubious, to the appraisal meeting. It occurred to me at the time, that there should be no surprises at appraisal time. It is no good saying to someone, six months after it was first noticed, that they use wrong sort of language in reports i.e. too negatively charged. In this situation, they have had six months longer to get it wrong. They will wonder why it hasn't been mentioned earlier and by storing up all their perceived faults, you will destroy their confidence and with it, any independence they might have begun to build.

The same manager had a slogan on his office wall. It read, *"Be reasonable, do it my way."* It was a value statement that he adhered to in his approach. In his own perception he was always right and had the confidence to carry it through; an accomplished workplace politician and negotiator. The trouble inevitably started, when the odd occasion arose (actually it wasn't that odd an occurrence), when he was wrong. He didn't have a slogan for that.

When people achieve, in a controlled and measured way, it is done almost without any obvious step change. It is only when you look back at the journey with them that they realise how far they have travelled. This is a great moment for them and for you as a coach, because it is a journey you envisaged, planned and helped them execute. You should be proud to have played a part in it. Don't fall into the trap though of changing the pace at which they are coached. Once you have found a pace which works for them and gives the optimum return, stick with it. If you try and overload them because they appear to be coping well with what you have given them already, you may undo all your good work.

With that in mind, think about the use of reports and statistics. Now I know that for some people, these are seen as the work of the devil, but if you can demonstrate to someone being coached, that the coaching has had a significant and positive impact on some aspect of their work, than you have already illustrated a great method of making the result of your coaching measurable.

In my early career, I used to travel around to the Company locations and complete standard audits, based upon annual objectives and certain administrative standards. The variance between sites, depending upon such factors as the ability of the individuals and the support they received from their managers was quite wide and, as such, the improvement levels also varied. I could have come up with a score for each section, based on my assessment, but that would have been fairly arbitrary. So instead, I started to introduce other factors; measurable indicators of their ability to complete key tasks. To do this, I had to work with and consult other areas of the business who interfaced with the locations; ones who had very specific key performance indicators of their own. It made more work for me, chasing down these statistics, pulling them together and presenting them, but it was well worth it. These particular measures were for such things as; annotation errors on delivery notes, late stock declarations, late order submissions, ordering products that were not officially listed etc. They were all elements which had a knock on effect if they were not completed on time or accurately and therefore their sensitivity and importance was amplified. The best aspect of the whole exercise was that you could then use another set of statistics to make some very valid observations and points. You could, for example, demonstrate where some locations were understaffed in their Administrative areas. If the ones which were consistently at the low end of the scoring, had fewer man hours and were not achieving and the ones at the high end had more man hours, and were hitting the standards, the point could be well made. Similarly, you could make a valid point about seniority levels and skill sets. It all worked pretty well.

So, I guess the point here is to think carefully about what it is you want to measure and where that data might come from, then engineer a way of pulling it together. In sport, for quite a number of years, coaches and managers have seen the value of statistics and data. In Football, for example, someone will watch matches on video and track a particular player. Each time the player completes an action; successful pass, failed pass, tackle, foul etc, the operator will stop the video and record the action on the computer. It will also track how much ground that player has covered during the game. Imagine the power that the complete data has, when put into the hands of a skilled coach. When he receives a report that shows that a player who is getting paid £80,000 a week, made seven complete passes, ran 3.5 miles and committed 4 fouls in a game, there is the evidence that the player needs some very specific coaching. Sure, you could pull the player aside and ask politely what value does he think he's adding, but wouldn't it be better to analyse the results and come back with some very targeted coaching, based on those and other statistics? In a game, just like the average day at work, you would never be able to log down all the indicators and measures available to you. Finding data elsewhere is a great way to support your coaching. This is not new or innovative reporting either. In the United States the American Football game use statistics like these all the time and have done for decades. How much yardage a player has made, how many intercepts, how many yards gained as Quarterback or receiver, as well as the obvious touchdowns or field goals scored. It gives us a measure of how that person is performing, against what we might expect to see.

The more you can measure, the more you can demonstrate improvement and assess the value of your coaching. You can see when something is working, what works and what definitely doesn't. There is a very important point here. It is not just about how well the coachees are doing in terms of your input and their ability to take on board the coaching. It is also about how effective you are as a coach. If you set the standards and harvest the measures, then analyse the results, it is you as the coach who first needs to interpret them and see if the buck stops with you. There is little point persisting with a particular angle of coaching or re-iterating particular points if the thrust of what you have been coaching is wrong. Perhaps the way forward is to discuss the data, in a positive way of course, and incorporate the views of the coachees into your analysis and ultimately the coaching points that come out of it. It may be that you will recognise that some of your coaching has been flawed either in its content or direction or it may even be that you haven't scaled the coaching properly, so that the improvement you were looking for was actually unrealistic.

2.3. What, How and When?

As a Swimming Coach, you have to plan a session, so that a balance is achieved. Over a period of time, each stroke and technique must be explored equally, to ensure that the swimmers receive an equal amount of coaching. What can alter that slightly is if one stroke or technique needs more work than another, but generally the view should be; don't just do breast-stroke all the time because it's easy. In planning a coaching session you will have definite coaching points, which you want and need to impart and a progression so that you can begin with something easy and build upon it. There is little value in expecting to describe or show, particularly inexperienced Swimmers, something complicated and expect them to just do it first time. It is not feasible, it is unreasonable and it is probably damaging.

By starting off with some simple exercise or activity, which may seem unconnected to the completed session, you can then add other activities and combine them, before bringing the whole piece together. In doing so, you enable the Swimmers to gradually build their skills. There is a great example of this concept in a well-known children's movie called the Karate Kid, where the Japanese Sensei has the boy cleaning his cars and painting fences in a rather contrived manner. The boy believes he has gone there to learn Karate and doesn't appreciate that his strength and motor skills are being developed in a particularly effective way. Once this is demonstrated, it is a revelation. It is also worth considering this; this is something I learned when coaching six and seven year old swimmers; simple is the most effective. That's why we break things down, often to their lowest common denominator. Napoleon made an observation that, *'The art of war does not require complicated manoeuvres; the simplest are the best and common sense is fundamental – From which one might wonder how it is Generals make blunders; it is because they try to be clever.'* If you start off trying to be too clever and devious in your coaching, you will confuse the message. Remember, it is about being able to take the coaching away and implement it. If it is too contrived or tricky, it will not be adopted.

I have seen 'coaches' in business offer coaching points in such a way that their charge is instantly over-faced. It would almost appear as if the coaching point is being offered as a token, rather than as an element of some more highly developed structure. You should never, as a coach, abuse coaching as an exercise you feel you *should* do. You will devalue the real meaty coaching that makes a difference.

When you are coaching in business, you should have some instinctive feel for it and be able to coach as you see, on the fly, but also you should structure and plan coaching to deliver the ultimate goals you have set. Sometimes the pressure of the job will mean that you are unable to coach what you want when you want to, but that is not always a bad thing, it will give the air of spontaneity to your coaching, rather than what appears to be a scripted and rigid programme.

You should also consider that in a live situation, when you have coached someone, they will generally be implementing the coaching points in a real environment. Unlike an athlete who may be able to practice techniques and try out your suggestions before a race or a match, in business it is *right now*. You might therefore, consider ways in which you could test the individuals on what they have been coached on in a relatively safe environment. An example you might use would be to get them to tell you how they would handle a particular situation or task, based upon the coaching you have given them.

Think of it this way. A tennis player may practice his drop shot a thousand times. In a match, he will not plan ahead, thinking 'I'm going to do my drop shot in six shots time,' It will not happen. Many factors will affect when that particular shot is executed. His position, the opponent's position and momentum, the mood or shape of the game at that time; is that drop shot going to break up a barrage of baseline to baseline deep drives? The coaching of how to execute the shot and the practice is one element of the deal. The remainder, and the most vital piece, is all about the when. If they get that wrong, they might as well have not bothered. In business it is just the same. Don't just coach how to do a particular thing or the approach they should take. Timing and situation are also important.

Another couple of great sporting comparisons come from Golf. A player reads the green in such a way that to play short will mean an uphill putt. The greens are playing fast, so the best thing to do is to hit just beyond the pin, but apply backspin so that the ball runs back toward the hole. In hitting that stroke you have avoided a difficult putt up the slope and the possibility of the ball running too far beyond the hole. In business you may coach people to do the same, in a variety of ways. You may suggest that a completion date for a project or job is given with contingency added in already, so that when you complete on schedule, it actually looks like you completed it early.

The second one is even more interesting, as it flies in the face of the fundamentals we have learned. Sometimes, if playing a short chip shot, the golfer's stance changes completely from the traditional stance. As an open stance increases loft and backspin, it can also help you hit the ball much higher than with a regular stance. This is because the hips rotate earlier in the downswing and the clubface is left open, this 'de-lofts' the face of the club. This can help you hit the ball over trees and other obstacles. You will typically see professionals take an open stance when they need to hit the ball a short distance, but very high.

So how can we equate that to our business world? The regular stance, gives us the distance, the accuracy and control we want, this approach gives us height, with a more open clubface and added backspin. Let's break it down.

I'm hitting high, to get over an obstacle or to avoid the ball running away on a fast green. I'm applying the brakes (backspin) to keep it tight and in a space where I want it to end up. I'm still in control, as I am using scientific principles, to apply the shot; it's just not the traditional method.

I suppose you could view this as an approach in business where you have a difficult situation and perhaps one where there needs to be an escalation to achieve the end result. You know that the regular approach will not deliver what you want it to, so you have to discard the conventional view. In your coaching you should prepare people for these situations. They may need to adopt a different stance on something to achieve a result. Spell out what the alternatives might be. Make sure they know what might work and what definitely will not work. Escalation does not always mean sacrificing organisational protocol, but it might mean knowing how best to manage your way through it. The approach play in business, like the approach play in golf, can often be the difference between an on PAR or under PAR score, or even a bogey.

I had a colleague who believed that, if he couldn't get his own way on something, he would simply copy a Senior Director in on an e-mail, where he would make his case again and reiterate how he believed this was the best way forward. It worked a couple of times. The senior guy intervened and let his line manager know that they should try it. Fair play then, he achieved what he wanted to achieve? Maybe that was the case, but it was really politically naive. After a few of these the Senior guy became a bit bored and sent the message back that he should follow the correct channels to obtain decisions and not always believe that he could just circumvent the process. At the same time and quite understandably, his line manager was a little miffed at regularly being both bypassed and overruled. It didn't make for a great relationship. A much better approach would have been to ask his boss to gain a second opinion and see what their Senior Director thought. This would be akin to the open stance. If the line manager was prepared to do that, this would be the backspin, getting the proposal into the target area, with the right amount of lift and power. It would have been a good precedent to set and would not have damaged his reputation. Furthermore, seeing that the Director supported the guy's views, it might even have encouraged a more open approach going forward.

2.4. Analysis – What did we do well?

Analysis of a piece of work, a project, or just the way we have approached a particular element of a job, can help us to do it better next time. Far too many people will just do a job adequately or in a close approximation to the timescales that have been set and be happy with that. If their manager is happy with that too, it reinforces a rather weak premise. If that is what happened in sport, then no-one would ever break records. The same people and teams would win everything and sport would become dull and pointless. Sports coaches will always analyse performance and look for the positives. It is important to take that view because those are the things which need to be reinforced. Take a golfer. He shoots a four over par seventy six, knowing that he is capable of an eight shot turn around on that to four under. Now that could be seen as a big negative, that he has gone eight shots adrift from his best, but if he simply focussed on what he has done wrong to get to that position, then that would dominate his thinking, his game plan and future rounds. He would concentrate so much on not doing certain things, that the things he had done well would be forgotten. It is the same in a piece of work. So, we did a good job but it was three days later than it should have been. What do we need to focus on next time?

The first thing to do when a piece of work is complete is to celebrate the positives. Just as a golfer might review his good shots and take confidence from them, we need to see and record what we did well in our work. Fine, we know we delivered it late and that was a negative, but perhaps in the positives we will find the reason why that was so. Had realistic targets been set, did someone not take account of the dependencies? This might sound like we are examining the negatives but think about it. An element of the work that was executed perfectly should be celebrated, even though it took eight hours longer than had been set aside, to achieve that level. That may need to be factored in next time, as a learning point. It might be that additional testing had been necessary due to unforeseen issues, which put the programme back further. Again, contingency may be added for next time.

To draw parallels, the golfer may have had some difficulties with a particular club that day. If it was excessively windy, hitting a wedge high in the air may not be the best shot choice. Even though the shots were hit straight and cleanly, the wind played a part in the accuracy. Might it not have been better to hit a club with less-loft short, and let the ball run, in conditions like that?

This shows a simple cycle of reviewing and analysing the current position, then targeting improvement, coaching through the improvement and allowing practice before reviewing again. The 'target' part of the cycle is highlighted, because this is where it can all go wrong. Coach the right thing at the right time.

In the diagram above, you can see the continuous cycle of coaching. You may wonder why we have a review and an analysis stage. When you review the practice or the piece of work, as a coach, you will be doing that with those involved, i.e. the team or the individual. The analysis is something you will possibly do yourself afterwards, taking on board your own thoughts and views as well as those of your team. You may then re-examine the target, whether that is a stage of a larger goal or project, or the ultimate goal. Our strength as coaches will be relative to our ability and flexibility. Remember to look for positives in the analysis that can be either expanded upon or adapted to take into other areas.

Do not try to analyse the game or the piece of work at the review stage. The review stage is for you all, coach and team, to discuss what occurred and how things played out, without any solutions, resolutions or next steps being discussed. Neither should there be any blame nor negativity. This needs careful thought and planning with other elements of the cycle. In the review, there may be some emotions, but these need to be worked through and out, before the analysis, as they do not form a part of that process. The analysis should be objective, free from emotion and target focussed. If you carry any emotional baggage into that part of the cycle you will not come out with good coaching points and a truly targeted progress plan.

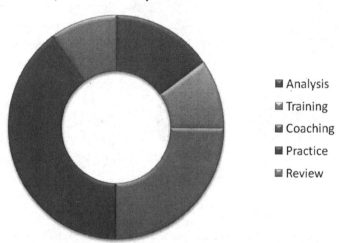

Cycle Element Proportions

- Analysis
- Training
- Coaching
- Practice
- Review

In the diagram, we can see the approximate split of elements in the coaching cycle. Analysis and training are very small parts, coaching and practice occupy approximately two thirds and review and analysis about a quarter. If you neglect the review, and particularly the analysis, you will begin the cycle again making the same fundamental errors.

The proportions shown in the diagram on the previous page are only an approximate guide and you could be more prescriptive if you wished. The idea is to illustrate that coaching occupies more space than training and approximately the same amount of space as review and analysis put together. By making review and analysis a very definite part of the cycle like that, you will ensure that the next coaching you do is properly balanced and targeted. You may also notice that the 'practice' or actually doing the job is about a third of the cycle. It's not a third of your team member's work time. Don't think of this cycle in terms of time, think of as the space that activity occupies. What is more important is that the actual coaching is a significant part of the whole process and not just a few cursory hints or tips thrown in to the working day in an arbitrary manner, just so you can say you coached. Always have a goal for yourself and them to achieve and always keep in mind what it is you are aiming to do.

2.5. Analysis – What did we not do well?

There is another very good reason to conduct the analysis away from those being coached. You don't want to go over the areas which were not executed well and make a big deal out of it. It may be that in the review, areas where there were issues were discussed, but don't let them dwell on them. Move on, and find a positive.

As a coach one of the skills you must develop, is a way of looking at negatives in a positive way. Take a Football coach whose team has just lost 5-3. You can't blame the goal scoring force, as they scored three away from home, that's a good thing. The defence is clearly lacking in some way, but what you don't want to do really is put the blame on them. Service from the midfield must have been good, to help get the three goals. So where are the positives to focus on?

- We scored three away from home.
- Midfield service to the forwards was good.
- We only let five in, it could have been worse.

Now, what are the negatives?

- We let five in.
- Support from the midfield to the defence was not great.
- We let the opposition attack us too much.

Now we need to turn those negatives into positives and then coaching points. There may be some more detail we can take from the game to support the positives, but just working with the basics we have here, we could start to engineer a positive spin.

- We need to take the game to the home side.
- Great attacking support, from the midfield, but just be wary of being caught out of position.
- When the midfield help out in the attack, don't lose your shape in defence.

For each of these you would then work out practice scenarios. It is difficult to steer clear of the negatives. It would have been too easy to berate the midfield for being caught out of position and the defence for losing their shape, but these criticisms must be avoided.

A similar approach could be taken in our business environment. A particular piece of work may have been completed, but it might be that it was completed late, over budget and additional expertise had to be brought in to complete some of the technical aspects. In the 'wash up', as a good coach, you have to remain positive, let's have a look and see what we can do to dissect it.

Positives
- The work was completed

Negatives
- It was delivered late
- We spent more than we budgeted for
- We needed additional expertise

Looking at the negatives positively:
- In spite of encountering difficulties and delays we completed the work to the standard required.
- A good practice in any piece of work is to add some contingency into the budget for unforeseen circumstances.
- In future what I would do is give the statement of work to a technical expert to review in advance of the work commencing, just to verify details.

The point should be made that the analysis is something you complete to come up with coaching points or hints, which will improve things going forward. You will already have had a review immediately after the work, which may have teased out some more positives about the way the job has been conducted, positive learning and anything which could be termed successes. Analysis will allow you to be more objective and choose your words carefully. A considered and reasoned analysis is far better longer term than a knee jerk and emotional response immediately after the job.

You will hear football team managers, being interviewed on the television after a particularly bad game say things like, 'We'll get the weekend out of the way then have a chat about it in training on Monday.' Clearly, what he is doing is letting the emotion drain out of the situation and allowing himself and the team some time to analyse what went wrong. This is a good thing. An explosive post-mortem just after a bad game would do absolutely no good at all and there would be fences to mend before the business of coaching could restart at the next session.

If you are analysing a poor performance, whilst remaining positive, ask the coachee to come up with ideas on how things could be improved, listen to them and comment as appropriate so that they know you are listening intently. Keep asking for their ideas until they have run out then offer yours.

You will find that approach a healthier and more productive use of your time than dwelling on the negatives and perhaps making your displeasure felt.

One other key factor to keep in mind, in relation to a poor performance, is something we have already touched upon. It is attitude of mind, but it can manifest itself in a number of ways, both in sport and in business. In a team game, like football, you might be playing against team from a lower division in a knockout competition and one or two team members might go into the game with the attitude that it is going to be an easy win. This is not a good point to start from. Bearing in mind that all the players in the opposing side will have the attitude that it is going to be a hard game and they are going to have to work their socks off. That is where the difference is going to be, not in skill, experience, not even talent, it is purely about attitude. Many times we see the so-called 'Giant Killers' who have caused an upset. It is no more than having the right attitude, right through the team. The difference in skill, between the teams as a whole, may be marginal once you add everything together. It only takes a couple of the team to drop their level by a few percent and the lower league side are in the ascendency.

In business we mentioned earlier a potential lack of diligence around mundane or administrative elements of work. Again this is all about attitude. When you complete your analysis, try to get inside the head of your team and gain an insight into how they might have approached the job mentally. Had you prepared them for it, had you fostered the right level of diligence? Make sure they understand that, there are no easy games. There are just those where anything less than 100% is not enough.

2.6. Points of Reference - The Model

A sculptor would generally have a plan, some sketches or even a model, before they started chiselling away at a stone block. You need a point of reference or a template to begin that process and in Sport and business contexts, there should be no difference.

You can't just pull a team together, or coach an individual in sport, without some guidelines to work with. Neither can you begin coaching in business, without first defining where you need to be. In fact it is a two-fold process. Where do I need or want to be? How do I get there? In chipping away at a granite block, the sculptor will know how to hit, where to hit, how hard and with what consequence, before each tiny tap. In our sporting context, the coach will have defined what it is they are ultimately trying to achieve and possibly worked out a number of key steps or stages to achieve that result.

In our examples we have talked about Golfers reducing the number of Strokes and Swimmers bringing down their times. So what are our points of reference in these cases? Is it the Professional Average Round, in golf? Is it the British or World record in Swimming? What do you think?

In my view, it is neither. They are all measures of achievement, which are fairly arbitrary. Many Professional Golfers will frequently beat PAR, in fact different courses have different PAR ratings, and they are therefore irrelevant as a model, just as the records of five or ten years ago in Swimming have no real relevance to a Seven year old swimmer now. Their goal, if they want to be World Class is going to be far quicker. The 'model' or point of reference has to be something which transcends those measures and yet is an anchor point, from which to correctly aim at our targets.

In swimming the point of reference has to be the four competitive strokes. They are the model we seek to achieve and develop an individual in their execution. It does not really matter how fast they become but the technique, skill and ability to execute them is the model we are aiming for.

Similarly in Golf, you could say that the model was the half dozen or so shot types, you may have to master, to enable you to play the game. Again, it does not matter how effective the player will ultimately be, but the shape they need to become in order to play is based upon their shot repertoire. If you think about it, the same is true in Tennis and other sports.

Therefore, it is no surprise that the model in business should have just the same basis in definition. It is those unalterable facts, seated within the execution of the role, which do not change, but perhaps become better executed or managed over time. Clearly these may change, from business type to business type, but perhaps we can put some generic markers down to help you establish your own individual ones. Here are a few which could apply to many roles.

- Security Policy
- General Discipline
- Dress Code
- Wastage Control
- Timekeeping & Attendance
- Communications – written and verbal
- Working Relationships
- Financial Controls
- Adaptability

Now you may argue that these bear no passing resemblance to the different shot types in Golf, or the execution of strokes in Swimming. I would disagree. If you think about what these are, they are the foundation level elements that apply to all our functions; some more than others and on top of which we can build other more diverse skill sets. If people are practitioners of these and follow the correct processes, they will set the right example, they will be perceived to be a solid performer, they will have the right mindset to get best value for your business and they most certainly will become influential members of the team.

Just as you wouldn't expect to throw someone into a pool and expect them to swim, or give a bag of clubs to someone and expect them to even be able to hit the ball, you would not expect anyone who didn't have some knowledge, understanding or operational grasp of these elements to survive very long in business. I'll give you what I consider to be a great example, from my own experience.

I inherited a member of the team from another area, when we had one of our many team re-shuffles. The person concerned had a great attitude, had established a good rapport with our particular 'customers' and was technical enough to wade through most of their issues, when on a site visit. The person had a friendly and down to earth personality, a sense of humour which gelled with those they dealt with and was generally well liked and perceived – externally – to be an asset. However, there were a couple of elements from the list above, that were not up to the standard required, to give the person the status they perhaps should have occupied. Written skills and verbal communications were neither fluent nor grammatically sound. Financial controls were *'someone else's problem'* and the general adaptability and acceptance of change to both process and environment was negligible. It was the equivalent of a Golfer turning up at the course with a bag of walking sticks, instead of clubs, teeing off from the greens and ignoring the 'out of bounds' signs. In terms of development, this person gave no indication that they could be developed; wanted to be developed, or how they might be developed, through coaching. I tried; believe me. In sculpture terms, I had a great block of marble, with some terrible cracks in it. I either scaled down my sculpture to something smaller, or had the whole thing ground into chips.

In the end it was the former, rather than the latter. We, both of us, had to accept that there were boundaries to where we could go as coach and coachee, but this conclusion was not based upon the skills or talents that person had, but the points of reference to which they need to be sculpted. It just was never going to happen. When we reshaped the teams again, and we promoted a peer above them, they were disappointed, but not surprised. At least I had approached that bit right.

I would like to say that, had I had access to that person from the start of their journey, I would have been able to engineer a better outcome. Although in this case, I don't think that is true. We are, sometimes, what we appear to be and if a broad understanding and acceptance of conformity and some self-awareness is not in your repertoire, it is hard to apply it, even with the assistance of a great coach.

To summarise, in this chapter we have looked at making small achievable corrections through coaching points, designed to chip away, much as a sculptor would, carefully targeting and executing those touches. We have discussed making achievements measurable and quantifiable, so that those being coached can see and feel the benefit of their coaching, without being outfaced or overwhelmed. We have looked at the value of analysis in the cycle of coaching and how and where that fits in, making sure that both the positives and the negatives are delivered as positively as possible. We have discussed what we should be coaching, how we should deliver it and when; not as a token or 'because I have to' but as a continuous and integral process. We have discussed starting off with a template or model that we want to coach towards and how that model should be constructed, based on global parameters in your sphere, as it is in sport and not just at a local level. In doing this and completing our coaching in this way, we will make our roughly hewn shape a more recognisable and more complete structure. In the next chapter we will look at turning that structure into something much more finished, polished and satisfying.

CHAPTER 3.
FROM SCULPTURE TO MASTERPIECE

In Chapter three we are now beginning to work at a much higher level. We are not only working with the pool of talent we have been given, but we have the opportunity to choose the people we work with. A coach in any field would have a much easier job, if they could always choose who they were going to coach. They could look for those with whom they felt the closest rapport and for those who would suit their coaching style. Importantly, if they could recognise, recruit and develop talent all the time, it would be a much easier job.

In sport, you can usually quickly gain a good idea where the talent is. Even in young children, just starting in a sport, a good coach will be able to spot the basics on which they can build. As we will see in a later chapter, in Football, it is the first touch. In a Swimmer, it might be their shape in the water. In a Golfer, it might just be a relaxed posture and swing.

A sculptor, might be able to create a better piece of work if he could afford a larger Studio, better equipment and tools and perhaps even a commission to produce a piece of work. The masterpiece would be borne out of the conditions these elements would create. In other words, given the access to better resources and freedom of choice, he would be better positioned to achieve his best work.

In the following pages we look at interviewing for talent, recognising it and developing it and then some of the tools and techniques we can use to keep that process going. In Britain particularly, there are certain sports where we have to wait decades for a really talented individual to emerge. Is that because at grass roots level, we are not recognising the potential of those who could become a great Tennis star, Sprinter or Golfer? In business, do we have the same issues? Do more people have the potential to be CEO or CIO level; we're just not recognising it and developing it?

Perhaps, in some instances, we are even ignoring it because it will take time and effort and it may be a bit of a gamble anyway. If sports coaches took that view, there would be no world record breakers; there would be no world class football stars that children will idolise. You have to take the view that every person whom you coach has the potential to be better than they are at what they do.

Hopefully, by reading and putting these things into practice, you will be in a much better position to identify those people, assess their potential and help create a few masterpieces yourself.

3.1. Interviewing for talent

I have interviewed quite a few people in my time for a variety of roles. I am happy to say that, with the odd exception, I have managed to recruit good stock. I put it down to instinct at first; it was something I believed I could 'sniff' out.

In sport, it appeared to me to be a little different. You could look for those basics I have either already mentioned or will cover later, first touch; balance and so on. In business what would you look for in an interview? As a coach in sport, you wouldn't begin to observe a potential athlete, swimmer or player, without first preparing and knowing what you were looking for. The same should apply in the world of work. You must prepare, ensure that you are absolutely clear on what is required and be prepared to work your way through the potential economies of truth, which are woven into the Curriculum Vitae. We have all probably heard of examples of how people have embellished their C.V. Subtle changes in the language can give a totally different picture. For example, 'Managed a small team', could actually have been one person. Be aware also that, just as you have prepared and know what you are looking for, the C.V. could well have been subtly re-engineered to relate more directly to the role you are interviewing for. In sport too, the 'Curriculum Vitae' can be a deception, if the scale of the achievement is not clearly stated. A boxer for example, who has won all his amateur fights on a knockout, may seem like a great prospect, until you actually realise that most of the people they have fought were relatively elderly punch-bags who had never won a bout in their careers. Then the record starts to look a little suspect.

When preparing for an interview in business, look for these potential embellishments in the C.V. and ask about them. Assess what sort of answer you get. It may help you interpret other things on the document, for what they are. Also look at the hobbies and interests? Try to establish more of a feel for who they are, rather than what they have done.

When it comes to the actual interview, the way you assess the individual will vary depending upon what it is you are looking for. Is it a person to fill a one off role? Is it a member of a team? Will they fit in with the dynamic of that team? Will they be able to work effectively alone? Just as a Football coach/manager might look for certain qualities when reviewing a striker, so you must look at how that person will perform in your team. In the case of the striker, the coach might look at the way he had scored goals in his previous team. Were they due to his work rate and endeavour, were they from great crosses? Can we provide those crosses?

As you might expect, I have a couple of examples from my own experiences. Let's take one where I was very right and one where I was very wrong.

I had the need to strengthen my team, working on the large project I have mentioned before. I narrowed the pile of C.V's down to three potential candidates. All three were in the right age group to fit the dynamic. All three had the right level of experience and had similar qualifications. All three seemed to have created a good work life balance for themselves. It was going to be down to the interview.

In the interview, in each case, I started by describing the role I was looking to fill, with an idea of the duties. There was some time away from home and a good bit of travelling. The main part of the role involved following a programme and being out on the road with very little supervision. I watched closely for reaction as I spoke about the role. Did people look excited about the challenges, were they daunted by them? Of the three candidates, this is what I observed.

Candidate 1. This person immediately followed up my description by saying they had worked away from home many times before and enjoyed travelling. They stated that in a couple of roles they had been in before, that they had worked from a project plan or programme and that, in some ways the roles they had performed previously were similar.

Candidate 2. Asked more specifically about how much travelling and how much time would they be away from home in the average week. They asked if they would be compensated for that time away from home and travelling time, if that was outside a normal working day.

Candidate 3. Described one of the roles they had done before, which seemed to fit nicely into the profile of what I had outlined, but was able to add substance and detail to that outline in a very ordered way. They said that they had sometimes set off the night before and stayed over places, to be there for an early start and they didn't mind that, adding that sometimes you had to accept that there were parts of a job which were sacrifices.

On those brief outlines, taking into account that they were all equally likeable and would fit into the team, which one do you think I chose? Which one would you choose?

Let's break them down.

Candidate 1. Was trying too hard to convince me that they had the right credentials and were not daunted by the travelling or staying away from home. I could guarantee that the role was not similar to the ones they had done before, the only similarities were in the travelling and the fact that it was prescribed work.

Candidate 2. Sought to quantify the travelling and the inconvenience factor and if there was any compensation for that. Having answered those questions – the answers were not important by the way – they were still interested.

Candidate 3. The fact that this person saw being away and travelling a lot as a sacrifice, was not necessarily a great basis for employment.

So, I chose Candidate 2. They were the most grounded, wanted to know the extent of the inconveniences and what they might get to compensate. They were still interested in the role having had those answers and were therefore, I believed, more likely to stay the course. It was that focus, that awareness of what could potentially be the least attractive part of the job that made up my mind. I knew they could all handle the work. It was these additional things which, over time, could wear you down, that had to be taken account of. Candidate 2 stayed the course and at the end of the project, took on a more responsible role. I called that one right.

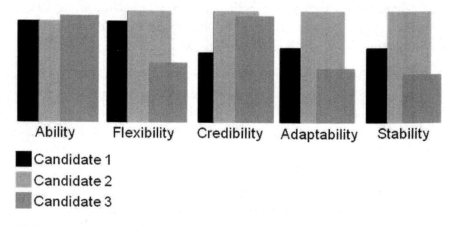

As can be seen above, although their abilities were similar certain aspects of their flexibility and credibility affected other scores. Imagine assessing three sport stars like this. You would be looking for a similar pattern and result to make a calculated choice. Use your own scoring mechanism (1-5, 1-10 whatever). I find 1-5 is adequate and gives enough scope.

The second example doesn't cover me in any glory. Again I was interviewing for the same roles as above and I had two candidates who were very strong. The first was a guy who had done a similar role for a competitor. He was older than others in the team, overweight and to my mind over-confident. The second candidate had a relevant degree, was very articulate and intelligent and was interested in a challenging future after the project had finished. I chose him.

What I hadn't taken into account was the team dynamic. His immediate team leader was a woman and quite a strong personality. After a while it became evident that; he wouldn't communicate with her, wouldn't take instructions from her, was frequently 'unavailable' when she called him on his mobile phone, had made enquiries about roles in other areas, having only been with us a month and so on. I had a chat with him, about his attitude and gave him a month to improve his communication and cooperation skills. They didn't improve. His position, in not communicating or being contactable, left us high and dry a few times and meant extra travelling and additional work for someone else. In his mindset, to take instructions from a woman in the work environment was completely at odds with his upbringing and culture. We parted company. The first guy, it turns out, would have been the better appointment. Someone I spoke with later mentioned his name and said what a great worker he was. I felt quite bad about it. You have to consider the dynamic, cultural fit and a number of other factors when making a team appointment. This is something that the five point assessment I applied earlier, would not have teased out, without an understanding and appreciation of cultural status.

There is also another factor that I was acutely aware of when I was pulling that team together. The project had a finite life and we were offering these people full time employment. They would not expect to be out of a job when the project finished. I had to blend different backgrounds and skill sets so that when retained, they would have very definite roles and be ready for development along with our growing department. I looked for skills we lacked overall as a team and deliberately had a leaning towards people who were different, rather than similar. Even though they were performing a similar role, I believed, and still do, that the dynamic should be as wide and varied as you can comfortably get away with. There are hidden bonuses to that. You will get a number of different viewpoints on the same issue, different solutions and suggestions. Once you have that kind of dynamic, it can be very interesting. It is a classic example of something that is greater than the sum of its parts. In the catch up meetings each week, they shared ideas, they showed how they had managed their way through issues and they gave each other advice and support.

3.2. Recognising talent

Some people go through life not realising that they have a talent, perhaps because they have never tried a particular activity or been in a particular role. There is a certain amount of trial and error involved in finding your niche and in finding a career that makes best use of your talents. You could blame the educational systems, for not identifying to individuals where their talents may lie, but that would be a little unfair. There is a whole world of difference between being a teacher and a coach. What I realised but probably didn't really assimilate at the time, was that at School, teachers actually coached best when they were running a non academic activity. Those who managed the Football, Cricket or Rugby teams; those who produced the School plays and concerts, were all 'coaching' when they put on the tracksuit or picked up a copy of Hamlet.

In effect, what they did was to take someone with a talent, or potential, and helped to add to that talent a skill. A skill is taught in, as we said earlier, you *teach in.* Once you have done that, you can begin to *coach out,* as the skill and the talent combine.

People may start with a talent, and have a skill imparted to them. The talent may be fairly raw, but have potential. By teaching in the skill and using their talent to harness and use the skill, we are putting them in a position where coaching can be successfully applied.

There is though, one fundamental question we need to ask first. What is talent? We can't possibly progress to recognising it in individuals, if we don't know how to define it.

A dictionary definition states it is: *'A special natural ability –or- A capacity for achievement or success.'*

In sport, if someone tries out a sport, as a coach you can usually spot talent pretty quickly, it's about those basics again. – First touch, body shape and position and so on.

In business talent is a little bit more difficult to quantify. People have tried all manner of tests and questionnaires designed to tease out the profile of an individual and identify where their strengths are. They don't always work. You have to be a little bit careful with these too. A little like horoscopes they can be right for 1 in 12 people. The more generic the result the more accurate it might seem. Neither does a talented individual always deliver to the expectations that may have been set by the 'identification' of their potential. We expect someone with talent to take on any task and complete it brilliantly; it doesn't always pan out that way. In business, as in sport, we must not lose sight of the fact that talent is also reliant upon circumstances or situations.

How many times have you seen a brilliant and prolific striker in Football, poached and transferred to another team, only to become less than average, his talent, seemingly drained by the move. What people have failed to take account of is that the service and supply he was getting at the initial club, played to his strengths. He was in a better position to use his particular talents and skills. Now, his current team are not geared to delivering the ball to him, how he can best use it.

The same can, and frequently does happen in business. So, what can we do to try to prevent this happening? Simply, we have to define the actual talent they possess and help the individual, through developing and coaching, to use it. For example, you wouldn't put a technically brilliant, but introverted engineer into a role where he had to interact with people all the time. Similarly, you wouldn't stifle a gregarious and extroverted character, by hiding them away in a programming job in a remote pod.

A sports coach will approach this as a matter of course, although the approach to an individual, working on their own in a sporting context, or a team player, will differ.

Let's go back to the diagram earlier in this section. Talent is an inherent thing. The skill taught to the individual should be related to and take the best advantage of that talent. You should therefore look at those you manage in a different way. Where do they seem to excel? What sort of things do they appear to enjoy doing the most and seem most natural doing? Make notes and at an appropriate point apply some analysis to what you have. What are the things that they do well and find easy, can these things be improved and honed? Do these elements fit naturally into a particular role?

Having talent does not necessarily make you a top performer. You need to be determined, dogged in your pursuit of excellence and either have the drive or be driven to achieve it. As a coach, you have to have the ability to, not only recognise the talent, but also get them to adapt what they have and apply the same principles to other, less well executed tasks or elements. This is where you have to break things down and understand why they are naturally good or gifted at something, then think of a way to apply those elements to the areas they, by comparison, struggle with.

So the question here really is, *'What do they find hard or difficult?'* You need to ask them why they think that is, rather than try to answer it yourself, even if you can see it. Once you know the why, you can start to assemble a coherent and achievable plan to address it.

The top performers in business and sport will share characteristics and traits. Tenacity, an unwillingness to accept that their personal best is actually the best they can do and a very goal orientated outlook. This makes them so much easier to coach, as they already have that mindset.

Just as sports people will look at improving by small margins, being strategic and, where relevant, tactical, the same will be true in the more successful business people.

As long as there are goals and targets to achieve in a longer term strategy, and they continue to achieve them, they will continue to persevere. Each day, they will set themselves little goals or targets that they must achieve and feel failure if they don't achieve them.

They will work hard, dealing with successes and failures in equal measure and not dwell on either in the pursuit of the next goal.

3.3. Developing talent

We have reached a point where we have identified an individual's talents and strengths. What we need to do now is to learn about them and what makes them tick. This is as important as knowing what they are good at because unless you find the key to unlock their learning and assimilation processes, you may waste a lot of time coaching them. Once again you should try not to think of coaching as being a subset of teaching; it isn't.

Teaching is about imparting a skill or a piece of knowledge. This knowledge may be used later, the skill may be something immediately put into practice, but coaching is not a part of that. Coaching is about bringing out of the individual, the talent and the skill combined and developing it to a whole new level.

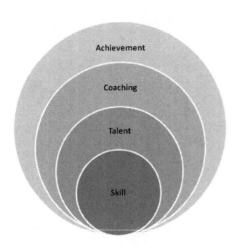

A skill can be taught. Basic coaching will take it to a particular level and more advanced and detailed coaching will take it to the next level. Achievement comes from continuing to work on the advanced coaching and developing the individual or the team to push harder and harder. People may start with talent and have a skill taught to them. Coaching takes the talent and the skill and combines them.

You are not teaching something with a coaching point, you are inviting those being coached to exercise their talent and skill and to add to it with a 'suggested' improvement.

They may take on what you are trying to get across, from a description, a diagram on a whiteboard, a demonstration or role play or by watching someone else, who can execute what you are trying to get them to do. The way they might get the message is unimportant. What is important is that you recognise how they got the message. If you do this, you will know for future reference the best way to deliver your coaching points and the most direct route of developing them.

How do people learn? – I can honestly say that, at School, I learned differently to most people. I had a good memory, evidenced by my ability to remember long passages in School plays, but some things in lessons just wouldn't stick. I realised years later that the way I best learned things was to break them down into their lowest common denominator and rebuild them myself.

Some people can read a book and take on board a skill. It is rare, but I have seen it done. Some people like being given the barest of data, then have a go themselves. Some will want to deconstruct the whole thing then build it back up again. Whatever the method the key to remember, as I have said numerous times already, you *teach in* and *coach out*. When you are dealing with the development of individuals, through coaching, you must remember that the way that it is coached out will vary and will depend entirely upon the way that individual assimilates and interprets the skill they are developing. This is an area you cannot 'clone'.

When I coached swimming I was conscious that the end result in each of the four strokes, and the racing dive, were very much accepted and documented. You wanted text book technique and you wanted to repeat that process with each swimmer that came through the scheme. How you achieved that though, would vary depending upon the individual, the point at which they started from and any other factors. For example, we often found that 'helpful' parents would listen to our coaching points and take them away to batter the children with later. Not a good thing. Coaching on some topics is quite often worthless out of context. Coaching someone on swimming technique in the car on the way home is very definitely out of context and will only confuse.

I found that some of the swimmers responded well to demonstrations by others who had mastered the technique, often of the same age or stature. Others needed to try it and be corrected; others needed to see coaching demonstrations like the alternating hand or arm movements. In rare cases, just outlining the mechanics and the end result of what you wanted them to achieve was enough. It was about taking their skill and the talent they possessed and through coaching, knitting those things together. I say knitting because it is a good analogy. The coaching is a continuous series of tight, linked knots, which will ultimately hold the whole structure together. Let us not forget though that with a pull in the wrong place or direction, it can be unravelled. Continuity in the coaching, the coach and the methodology employed is a key here. You wouldn't change your needles for a different size half way through a pullover, would you? I don't know enough about knitting to comment, but I'm guessing you might not.

In business it is just the same. People learn differently and respond or are motivated differently. Obvious coaching may turn some people off, whilst overly subtle coaching may be just too subtle for some. You have to find that balance and be consistent in the way you coach individuals. If it's a team you are coaching, you can be a bit more generic, but stay clear of making points which appear to target some individuals within the team.

I had two members of staff who worked with me a few years ago. They were similar ages, from similar backgrounds and both pretty technical in terms of their abilities. They were as different as chalk and cheese though and had to be handled as such. One, let's call him Andy, was reticent, quiet and would check everything before he did anything. The other, let's call him Bob, was a little too quick off the mark sometimes and would quite often dive in without thinking. You could not possibly coach them the same way. In simple terms it was a case of 'brakes off' for one and 'brakes on' for the other. I had to think carefully about how I did this because I didn't want to de-motivate either of them.

In swimming I recalled two kids who came to us from the same school. One was a thrash and splash merchant, the other cautious and considered. I pitted them against each other in a race, just 25 metres and thrash and splash ran out of steam at the 20 metre mark, allowing young Master 'considered' to take the spoils. I decided to adopt a similar strategy with the two employees, with one subtle difference. I put them together on the same little project and in the 'coaching' briefing I said to them, "You two have different styles and approaches. I want you to work together and come up with the result, using your combined strengths." Then I outlined how each worked and what I felt were the plus points of each approach. What I didn't do was to explore the down side of each approach.

They completed the job, but not without some minor frustrations. Bob would be straining at the leash to do things and move on, Andy would want to double check that they were on the right track. Gradually, with some input from me along the way, they both gravitated towards the middle ground. Bob would check things and test things first and Andy just became a lot faster and more decisive. They were still quite different in the way they approached and handled tasks, but they had learned some really valuable lessons from each other. For the record, Bob moved on and is now a team leader in I.T. at a well known organisation and Andy left us to do a post graduate PhD; two great guys.

Generally, sports people are more goal-orientated in their approach. It is not just about reaching a standard and achieving it. It can be about achieving it at a specific time and date. Performance in sport is very much about when and where. In our business context, sometimes the goals can be less fixed and less time bound. We can learn a great deal from sport by being a little more time focused and perhaps setting smaller, easier to achieve goals or steps, but have more of them. By doing this, we will not necessarily outface the person or team we are coaching. For example, you wouldn't take a relatively talented Golfer with a handicap of eleven and set them a goal of achieving scratch in six months. If you did, they would probably set individual goals and targets to achieve that, which were unrealistic and which wouldn't work. Instead, you might set a goal of reaching a handicap of nine in a month's time, down to seven in another six weeks and so on. In that way, they would be able to look for the key areas where they can improve and save shots. Similarly, in business we should be more graduated in our approach. If you set a goal with a member of your team to save £100,000 in operational expenditure in the year, it may have them looking for that one killer saving that will achieve most or all of it. Break it down and set more staged savings and they may have more success.

There are many people in business who are busy doing nothing. Sports people are never 'busy'. Instead they are focusing on performance. Being busy does not necessarily bring with it results or performance, being absolutely performance driven does.

Don't just think about solving problems or putting things right. Look at the talent and skill of the individual and the opportunities those things present, coach upwards from that point, not up to that point, from a position of rectification. When you give them coaching points avoid giving them as if you were giving advice. What would work better is if you could impart information to them, which they can use to improve themselves. We briefly mentioned earlier (2.5.) about using the 'What I would do...' approach. Try and combine these approaches, in which case you might say, 'Given that information, what I would do is....' Let them make their own choices, but from an informed position.

You should never over train someone or over-coach them. Training can become tiresome if it is constant and requires assimilation or absorbing. Equally too much coaching can become as destructive as none at all. In both you should allow time for the individual or team to deal with the coaching points and training and see some benefit from it. In the case of coaching, the overload can happen purely by trying to coach too much at once. It is good to keep coaching and improving by degrees, but too much in one hit should be avoided. There is no rush. Similarly, with feedback, keep it contained. At most, give them three things to work on and three things to keep doing. Many coaches make the mistake early in their tenure of needing to find things wrong and identify them. It's the old, *'Look at how clever I am to spot that,'* routine. It's not really necessary. In working that way they can become entrenched in being very critical and not giving out enough praise. Some coaches even advocate that you should find ten things they did well and focus on three of them, making the coaching points meaningful. Others state that you should ask the coachee what they want to work on. It is whatever works best in each situation, but the key thing to remember is to remain positive. Certainly, if they can identify their own weaknesses and areas for improvement, you will get a better level of engagement from them when you coach on it.

You should never bring luck into the equation. Luck is not something you can quantify; therefore it has no place in coaching. I personally do not believe in luck of any kind either. There are statistics, chance and the law of averages, which cover some of the occurrences attributable to what some people may call luck, but talent, skill and hard work have nothing to do with it. There is a great quote attributable to (amongst others) Gary Player, the golfer, it goes something like this.

I was practicing in a bunker down in Texas and this good old boy with a big hat stopped to watch. The first shot he saw me hit went in the hole. He said, "You got 50 bucks if you knock the next one in." I holed the next one. Then he says, "You got $100 if you hole the next one." In it went for three in a row. As he peeled off the bills he said, "Boy, I've never seen anyone so lucky in my life." And I shot back, "Well, the harder I practice, the luckier I get."

Inferring that someone's ability, talent or perseverance is nothing more than just 'luck' is at best insulting, at worst demoralising, but either way de-motivating. In a sporting environment, people have been heard to say you make your own luck. This isn't luck at all; it is talent and skill making the best of opportunity. You only make your own luck in this context by training hard, being well coached and by being a good practitioner. If everyone relied on luck, as some sort of ill-defined and 'spooky' power, then no-one would try as hard as they do. There would be those who believe they are lucky and those who don't and their approach would determine the outcome. If I were a golfer, hitting consistent five under par rounds, come rain or shine, that wouldn't be because I was lucky, I can assure you.

Similarly, successful businessmen are generally so because they can spot opportunities, they are innovators, they have skills and talents and they often take calculated risks. Don't ever believe that they are or have been lucky.

3.4. Talent matrix

The primary purpose of the talent grid is to define where a person is currently placed in relation to their potential. This will help us to determine the next course of action to help them move up or right on the grid to better themselves. The grid should be used objectively and without any comparison to other individuals.

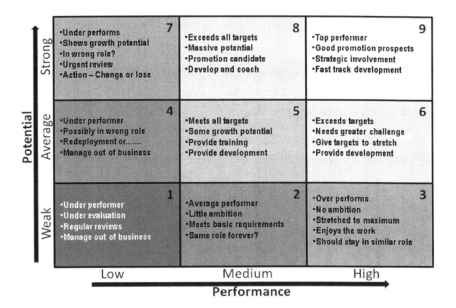

This is one variant of the Talent Matrix; you could engineer your own. The main feature is the progression from bottom left to top right, where the X axis is gauging potential and the Y axis illustrating performance. The focus here is on the amount of input, effort or coaching you want or need to put into them.

Box 1 - Under Performer – Under evaluation – Regular Reviews – Manage out of Business.

In the case of someone whom you assess to be at this level, you should put more effort into managing their day to day performance than trying to develop or improve them. There should be an action plan to help them see what the specific goals are and they should be in little doubt about what is required. You should make sure that you document and clarify what it is that you want to see them do.

That conversation should not be one way. You must encourage them to discuss what they feel could be preventing them from performing to the required standard and don't give the impression that they have little potential. If you can, you must then remove the elements that they believe are blocking them.

In the performance plan, be very explicit about how you want them to perform and what you will be looking for as indicators. Give them regular feedback, not on a schedule, but as and when you see things. Don't just point out the bad stuff and go over the same ground either. Make it positive and make sure the feedback is balanced.

You should never write someone off without giving them the opportunity to respond to your targeted input. Between each of you, decide upon what is a reasonable amount of time to improve and outline what the consequences might be if the targets set are not met. You may even reach agreement, through this type of consensus, that they are not suited to the role.

In sporting terms, this person doesn't want to play for the team, or isn't of the same calibre as the others.

Box 2 (average performance, limited ambition)

I suppose you could call a performer like this 'steady away'. You know exactly what you are going to get out of them and whilst it is a reasonable and acceptable job, it is never going to be more than that. They are quite happy to come in and do their work to the standard required, and do not really have any ambition to push themselves to achieve much more than that. Neither will they respond very well to being 'pushed'. Unlike Box 1, they are suited to their role and it should be tailored to suit them. Bear in mind that you cannot force someone to be dynamic or to want promotion. What you can do though is make sure that they take pride in their work, coach them to maintain consistency and introduce new tasks or changes that compliment what they are doing.

In sporting terms, a solid defender who does a job but never really fires the imagination.

Box 3 (high performance, limited potential):

At this level you should determine what motivates the person and try to gain an understanding of how they want to develop. You should give them opportunities to develop in the role they occupy and make sure that they are challenged and can expand their capabilities and knowledge. Make sure that you encourage them frequently and where possible reward their endeavour. You should also make sure that they are clear about their prospects for advancement, if they ask, and look for indicators that they may be thinking about moving on. If this looks like a possibility you may wish to have them mentoring others or coaching junior members of the team. They are likely to be knowledgeable and 'experts' in what they do. Allow them to share their skills and experience in presentations etc. Make sure they feel valued and respected. Do not neglect their coaching just because you feel they have limited potential.

In sporting terms, someone who tries very hard but whose work ethic exceeds their talent.

Box 4 (acceptable performance, moderate potential):

A person in this category could be classed as an underachiever. However, they may be in the wrong role and with the correct input and feedback, their potential could be realised. Again you should make sure that they are clear about their prospects for advancement. It may be that your grading structure and scales will allow movement in their benefits and rewards, but these will clearly depend on their ability to respond. A well defined programme of performance management, coupled with coaching and appropriate training course should begin to reap benefits. This may take their 'acceptable' performance to a good or better than average level. If they are not prepared to move roles, perhaps you might consider losing them.

In sporting terms, in the position they occupy, they might work out in a lower division, but never the Premiership.

Box 5: (good/average performance, moderate potential):

This person could go either way. They are already providing an average performance and have the potential to better themselves, but are not necessarily enthusiastic about it. You shouldn't push them to want more in advancement terms, but equally their input should be geared to allow for it. People are allowed to change. They should be continually given opportunities to push themselves or test themselves outside of their normal comfort zones and will probably relish those challenges. Occasionally you should try to stretch them, whilst providing any coaching or nurture they need. They may have to be convinced that they can achieve more. Let them know that their reliability and results are valued, get them to contribute ideas and listen to them. Trust their judgement; go out of your way to ask their opinions. Make sure they get credit for a job well done.

In sporting terms, they might be one of those Golfers who is always around the top 10-20 players but never bags a title.

Box 6 (high performance, moderate potential):

These people have the capability for higher profile or more demanding roles, but are not quite ready. Their performance standards are generally very high and this should be built upon. They should be coached and encouraged to try new things which take them out of their current role and comfort zones and stretch them. There should be an element of raising their profile, by giving them high value or exposure tasks. You should perhaps also look at giving them something ground breaking or innovative to do; something which they take from start to finish. They should also be exposed to an assignment which is a business problem or to put right something which has been done badly by someone else. This will all serve to develop their potential in readiness for longer term opportunities. You may also consider a job swap, an opportunity to experience a new role, in an interim capacity.

In the sporting world this could be a Cricketer who needs to move up the batting order or a solid team player who should be handed the captaincy.

Box 7 (poor performance, high potential):

It's very likely that these people are in the wrong role. Here is where you need to break down their performance and analyse it against their strengths and weaknesses. Once you have the root cause of their under-performance, work out an action plan to rectify those weak areas and even consider moving them to a role which plays more to their strengths. It might be that they just need more coaching or a mentor to help them through. You might even consider a combination of approaches, depending upon the individual or their role. You might want to consider exposure to high performers in your team, so that they can learn a different approach; even those with less potential than you assess they have themselves. Sometimes it is just requires a trigger to switch on that improvement you seek. After a reasonable length of time, if there has been no improvement, you might want to make a re-assessment of their potential.

In sporting terms you might have a middle distance runner who needs to move up to half and full marathons. Paula Radcliffe for example, had limited success at Cross Country and middle distance, but when she moved up to the longer events, even 10,000 metres, she was world class.

Box 8 (good/average performance, high potential):

There should be very little difference in the way you approach these individuals from the way you approach Box 9 individuals. All you are looking for is an increase in performance and in some competencies that will plug the perceived gaps. Provide some stretch assignments; easy does it at first. Try to give them something rare or groundbreaking to do. Analyse any weaknesses or competencies that need improvement and get them to come up with ways to address that. You need to get them from good to great. Know the difference and try to get them to understand what that difference is. It can be adjustments rather than massive changes, subtle and cumulative.

In sporting terms, a world class Tennis player, just outside the top five. It's going to be about a few weak shot types, their approach to the game and perhaps their mental attitude.

Box 9 (high potential, high performance or hi-po as they are called):

Provide these high performers with stretch assignments; opportunities to learn new skills and new areas that take them out of their core competencies. Give them something to do where there is a definite challenge and the result is critical. You could maybe look at something new or innovative, perhaps a piece of work that aims to fix a long term problem or issue or just to clean up after a bad job done by someone else.

Help them to build a network of their peers, so that they can exchange views and ideas and build relationships. You might consider giving them an interim role at a higher level to let them grow and demonstrate their flexibility and adaptability.

Don't neglect their training, coaching or mentoring just because they are in the higher echelons of achievers. Keep feeding the flames, but watch closely to make sure that you don't overload them. Make sure you are aware of their potential to move on and leave your business. Keep the focus on developing their profile and exposure. Make sure that they can and do interact with the higher levels of the organisation.

In sporting terms they are at the top of their game, a hot property, talented, in demand and marketable. Keep them happy and busy, keep them challenged and ensure they receive the recognition; keep them.

3.5. Skills Matrix

One of the key aspects of understanding the dynamic of a team, or even an individual, is to construct a skills matrix. Basically, for each individual you are coaching, list down their skills. It may be that a few people have the same skills, so this is how the matrix is constructed. You can see who has what skills, and who perhaps needs input or training, or even, when looking at a project, it will allow you to select the best mix of people to cover all the bases. The matrix might include what experience they have in each area of skill.

However, experience may not actually matter as long as the people have the right skills you are looking for.

I have a prime example of this from my schooldays. Before diving into the anecdote, a little insight into why the above statement is important. You have to assess what it is you are actually trying to achieve. Now, this can change, over time. It doesn't have to be the end game, but you must have a goal in order to be able to determine how and why you are coaching. In selecting a team, it might be about horses for courses.

In the sixth form, once our final examinations started, we had technically, if not legally, finished school. Quite a number of people took that opportunity to begin their summer holidays early and the numbers of those who turned up for extra-curricular activity diminished rapidly.

In that year, I had been nominated and elected Vice Captain of House. Our school had four houses; DeLacy, Hook, Oastler and Priestley. I was in DeLacy and we had been successful in winning the house championship in the last three consecutive years. A position our House Master did not want to concede. The major perk in winning the Championship was that you were allowed to use the main School hall for your house assemblies. It was a status thing, but also much better than 25% of the school being crammed into one of the larger Labs or Classrooms.

As we approached the final events of the term and the final Soccer competition, we were running the title extremely close with Oastler. In fact, it would all come down to who won the Soccer competition, which was a simple league table. We won the first two games, Oastler had won one and drawn one, we were then set to face each other in the final game, which would determine not only who won the Soccer, but the House Championship! It was all very exciting. At least, it was all very exciting for those of us left. As I spoke with the House Captain, it came out that he – one of our best players – would not be available and neither would several other key team members. A little sniffing around, on my part, made it clear that the opposition would be at full strength. It would be left to me to pick the team. I double checked the scores and found that, if we only drew, we would win the football and also the championship itself. I had to work out my strategy and try and pick the team accordingly, although not necessarily in that order. I knew only one thing; defeat was not an option.

Now, it came to pass that we could use potential players from the year below us, if they were interested. I started to look at whom we had available and what their football skills amounted to. I began to despair a little, as there were quite a few Rugby Union players, but not many who were confident and keen on the spherical ball. I thought about the opposition. They were largely decent players. They had one or two that were quick, but who were light and small. They didn't have any real bruisers in their team. I decided that my strategy would be to build a fearsome midfield and defence made up largely of scary Rugby players and one guy who could have passed for a bulldog had he been a little more hirsute. As far as coaching went, I brought them together one night for some training and to finalise their positions. My one and only coaching point was, 'I want you to scare the hell out of them.' There were a few nods of approval and grins at this, so I added the caveat that this should be done within the laws of the game.

The game itself was quite a treat for the spectators. It was end to end, full of incident, but surprisingly, for a school game, goalless. The nearest anyone came to scoring was when I grazed the bar with a free kick. Apart from that, we made it, we won the Soccer tournament and with it the championship. It felt great.

I suppose the point is that sometimes you have to define what it is you want to achieve, once you know what skills you have available. You can't always set out with a goal and Coach the team or individual into delivering it. Had I set out intending to win the game, my team choice may have differed and the coaching may have been more specific. In doing so and creating a false ambition, I may have ended up losing the game. This is where a Skills Matrix can be very useful in coaching; especially in the team situation. If you have a matrix showing people's skills and strengths, you can more easily examine whether they can be better utilised or question if the way in which they operate can't be modified to take advantage of those strengths.

It is also about the way you coach people, based upon their strengths. You can look at a particular skill or strength, or even an attribute, and by determining how that skill or strength manifests itself in the individual, how they acquired it and how they have developed it, use that as a model to develop other areas in need of nurture. You must remember though that you cannot fit a square peg in a round hole. There are some things that you may improve, but never really consider to be top class. Just as in sport, there are people with different types of muscle fibre for sprinting, or for endurance, in business there are those who are great at the quick, simple straightforward tasks and those who relish a marathon.

The Skills matrix allows you to scale coaching – Because you have identified a person's potential and where they currently are in relation to that potential, you can scale their coaching and development accordingly. You can target the areas you need to focus on more effectively and with a purpose which is not singly job or project related, but more developmental.

Below is a typical skills matrix you may have in a particular function or team. Down the left are the core skills for the whole team and across the top, the names of the individuals in the team. You simply put a cross to populate the matrix to show who has a particular skill.

Skills Matrix	J Jones	L Munro	G Barrie	D Lester	A Defoe
Financial Controls	X			X	
Administrative Skills	X			X	X
Customer Service		X	X		X
Communication		X	X	X	X
Line management	X	X	X	X	
Technical Skill	X		X		X
Project Mgmt	X	X	X	X	

This matrix now has a variety of uses. You can use it to identify skills gaps, i.e. 60% of your team do not have any skill in financial controls. You might, therefore, schedule them some training and then plan their coaching to help them use the acquired skill and knowledge in the work context.

You may have a senior role to fill and be looking for someone with financial and administrative skills as well as line management and communication skills, in which case D. Lester is an ideal candidate to have a closer look at.

It may be that you are simply looking for a technical project manager to look after and help implement a new system. In which case, J. Jones could probably hit the ground running. You may even consider tagging A. Defoe along with him to help with the Administrative, Customer Service and communication piece and to learn about Project management and the financial management of a Project.

Your skills matrix may have many more skills and more specific ones aligned to your department, business or products you use. I have seen ones which go down to the level of skill working with specific devices, software packages and methodologies. There is nothing wrong with that as it immediately ticks the boxes of the examples we have discussed. If you were planning to introduce Microsoft Office into a new area of your business and you could see that only two people were MCSE qualified, you might want to address that first.

You are enabled to look at your team or individuals in a completely different way. Not only being able to identify where they need input and work, but also where they can become useful in your coaching sessions. They could share their skills and knowledge in mentoring others. They could assist you in putting together presentations or detailed report packages. In effect you can use their current skills at a higher level, developing them further and allowing them to make a greater contribution.

3.6. T.A.S.K.

In the late eighties and early nineties, I was involved in I.T. Training for a few years. There were a few processes you could use to determine what training people required, such as TNA (Training Needs Analysis). I found that they didn't quite do what I wanted them to, because they focussed on identifying skills gaps and then formulating the training that people needed to plug those gaps. This was all very well, if you were just looking at providing training to complete a number of set tasks, such as developing a spreadsheet or completing a word document.

A well known and respected training author and specialist at the time, Colin Corder (sadly deceased), wrote a book entitled, 'Teaching Hard, Teaching Soft', which I found very useful. It made me patently aware that we were only examining the 'hard' skills, those that could be taught from a book or on a device in a processed way. The soft skills were I felt, more important. They were more person to person dependent, whereas the hard skills training would be the same, no matter what the group dynamic was. I decided that I should pull together my own assessment method, for the staff I dealt with. I called this system T.A.S.K. (Training, Attributes, Skills & Knowledge). The idea was to be able to assess an individual's suitability for a particular role and for the next step up, by assessing where they were and what input they may need to get them there. I found that these key elements also had a relationship with other components of a framework where the Person, the Input and the Output were towers, connected by a logical progression. If we look at an individual in relation to these elements and examine these towers we will gain a better understanding of how we might coach the person.

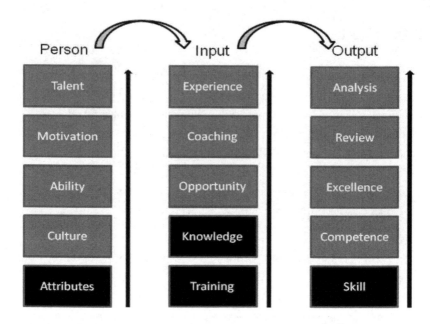

The diagram above indicates the relationship between the different elements we should consider when looking at coaching. You can see how the components of T.A.S K. span the towers and underpin the framework.

Person
A persons potential, without any further input can be described by the first tower.
Their attributes are pointers to what sort of person they are; confident, outgoing or naive, introverted and so on. Knowing and understanding these will put you in a great position to develop them further.
The culture out of which they have been borne will have an impact on how they will interact with others and, how they might respond to different groups of people.
Their ability, right at that moment, is not about their talent, don't confuse the two. Their ability may be limited at that point because they have not had the required input.

Their motivation is one of the defining factors and will have a direct impact on how far they will go, once they have begun to be coached. There are many reasons and circumstances why and how much someone may be motivated.

Then of course there is their talent; their *special natural ability* or *capacity for achievement or success.* It may be that their ability, also mentioned in this tower is seemingly unrelated to their actual talent. Many great musicians are also reasonably good artists, which one is driven by their ability and which one is driven by their talent?

Input
The second tower is about what we can add to the person, to improve their performance and help them to achieve their potential.
Knowledge is always a good yardstick to judge someone's interest in their environment and to gauge whether they will respond to training and coaching. It might be that you assess this by some form of test or aptitude assessment, but don't use this as the absolute measure.
What training have they had already? Has the training been relevant to what they appear to have a talent for, or has it been given in an effort to knock a peg into the wrong shaped hole.
Probably the single most important element in this tower after coaching is opportunity. A person with the ability, talent and skill to become a great Tennis Professional might never get the chance to play on a Tennis court. Opportunity is what gives someone with ability the chance to exercise their talent.
Coaching is the whole purpose of this book and the whole purpose of this tower. It is what connects the People tower to the Output tower. Without it, knowledge, training, opportunity and experience do not have any relativity. A person with all these other elements in place could practice for years, without any significant improvement.
All the talent, ability and opportunity, in the world, needs to be pulled together and experience is the medium which allows that.

Output

The output, in all its forms is what we start to see when someone begins to achieve their potential.

What skill or skills a person has can vary greatly and the skills link to a talent can also be irrelevant. In assessing someone's skills, it is worth doing so in consideration of their inherent talent. It may be that these could be adapted to help develop that core talent.

Coaching an ability or skill and developing a talent will lead to competence. This is a level at which you can tell whether an individual has the true potential to gain the best out of their talent and can maintain consistency, over a period of time.

The next stage up from competency is excellence. Competence can really be defined as a base level, in which everything is 'acceptable', where excellence is more about finesse.

It is only when this tower is activated that review becomes both necessary and structured. Review is mainly about the individuals' view of their performance, with some small contribution from the coach.
On the other hand, analysis is the coaches' way of turning critique into coaching. It is the final point in the cycle, before we return to the central tower again. You should not undertake analysis whilst coaching, it will almost certainly not be objective, it will contain negative elements and you will not be able to convert your thoughts into useful coaching quick enough.

If you look at those towers again and think of them in relation to a sports academy or coaching school, they will address all of those elements, whilst they improve a person's sporting abilities. Good coaches will, without even realising it, improve the person as a consequence of coaching them to be better sportspeople. It is the discipline, the attention to detail and the positivity which will trigger all manner of developmental threads.

Going back to the original point, the hard skills only really affect two of the boxes in the towers. All the others are soft skills or 'soft' subjects, where more understanding is required. It really underlines the fact that you need to know the people you are coaching and know how those important elements all have a profound effect on the end result.

If you take the output from the talent matrix and the skills matrix and then apply the T.A.S.K. principle to them, you can begin to accurately construct and target individual and team development. You don't have to do it this way; it will just help provide continuity and a solid base from which to work.

3.7. Inspire by example

Those who inspire us, as people doing a job, coaches, sportspeople, are generally people who possess something just a little different.

It can be at several levels. I have encountered people who have inspired me as teachers, as supervisors and managers, or even business leaders. It is not necessarily about their own personal success either, it can simply be the way they approach and deal with things. What is inspiration after all? The dictionary definitions vary, but the simplest seems to be - *Stimulation of the mind or emotions to a high level of feeling or activity.* If you can trigger that sort of response by inspiring someone, or be inspired by someone, that is generally the outcome. It is therefore, by definition, a form of coaching.

I had a friend who coached a relatively successful Football team. He called me up one day with a bit of a problem. It seems he had a guy playing for the team, a midfielder, who had been on the books of a Premiership Team, as a junior. They had let him go due to an injury he sustained, which had since been fixed. He was head and shoulders above the other players, not just in the team, but in that particular league and could have played for anyone. The reason he had joined their team was because he was from that area.

The problem was that the player always turned up late for training and sometimes not at all, but because of his skill, my friend couldn't afford to leave him out of the side. There was a danger that other members of the squad would perceive this as 'special treatment' and start to feel resentment, even though; once at the training sessions, he worked harder and longer than the others, frequently staying afterwards with half a dozen balls, hitting them at the empty goal, or taking himself off on a three mile run. My friend was concerned that if he tackled him on his timekeeping and attendance, he would simply go elsewhere.

I could see my friend's dilemma. At work, I once had a similar situation. A member of my team was generally late for our normal start time but stayed well beyond the standard finish time; a fact that few would actually see. All they would see was him arriving late and not being picked up on it. It was all about perception. After some thought, I gave him a particular task to own which meant that he had to be in earlier, but which gave him a greater sense of responsibility. He was never late again, thus changing the perception, but without having to have any badly managed conversations about how he might be viewed.

My advice to my friend was therefore quite simple. Why not get the star to help coach and select the team? Draw him out and give him more of a sense of ownership; he has seen how premiership sides train and coach players, perhaps he could bring some of that to coaching his team? It would change the perception, improve the way the team was coached and, make them feel like they were let in on Premiership coaching secrets. It would make him feel like his value to the team was actually greater than being 'just another player'.

My friend took the advice away and things changed immediately. He was never late again, made a significant contribution to the team's fitness and core skills, actually played better himself; was more of a team player than prima-donna, and a few years later, when my friend retired from the Coach role, he took over completely and the team prospered even more, going on to win several trophies.

The lesson here is two-fold. Understand all the possible dimensions of what potential you have in the people you coach. There may be the opportunity for better utilisation staring you in the face. Also, there are no difficult situations you cannot handle sensitively, with a little structure and thought.

One of the best managers/coaches I have worked for did so mostly by example. He was a Warehouse Manager and ex-guardsman, named Alan, whom I encountered early in my career. I was one of four Supervisors who reported to him. His style was very much one of clear, unambiguous instructions and creating an atmosphere of calm and control. He could assess, analyse and decide very quickly what needed to be done without any flapping or drama. I guess that was his military training coming out, think fast, and react. If there was a job to be done, he would be the first in there, energetic and involved, but at the same time encouraging others to share the experience. I learned a lot from him about a calm approach. If you take a step back and have a look at the whole picture, you can see a lot more and pick the right solution. Those few seconds of clear thought, in any situation, can make the difference between a winner and a loser. One great example, I recall, was in the lead up to Christmas one year. One of the other Supervisors had stacked three pallets of carbonated drinks; lemonade, cola etc, on top of each other at the end of an aisle. He hadn't put any sort of barrier in between, such as cardboard and despite warnings, the inevitable happened. One evening as we tidied up from the days efforts, there was a cacophony of sound from that particular aisle. The manager and I moved quickly to it, to be faced with a Tsunami wave of fizzy drink heading down the warehouse. Alan looked at it and calmly said, *'Go and get the floor machine and ask one of the lads to bring a few cardboard boxes a brush and a shovel for the glass.'* There was no change in tone, no panic, no frustration, just a very quick clear assessment of what needed to be done and what was required to do it. When the floor machine arrived (this was a big floor cleaner with brushes and a vacuum for the water) he took control of it and hoovered up the lake of fizzy pop, taking care to avoid any glass. I reckon there were around 200 two litre bottles smashed in that incident and it was all cleaned up and sorted within 30 minutes.

Alan would always give you positive feedback too. It may have occasionally included a recommendation to try things slightly differently next time, but it was always positive. Even the supervisor, who had stacked the pallets of fizzy drinks, had a positive dialogue with him about it. Alan took the blame and said that he should have overruled it and had the pallets moved and that you learn from your mistakes. I can think of few managers, who were around at the time, who would have taken a completely different view.

There must be people, either from your education or career to date, or even your private life who have inspired you by their example. Don't forget these instances in the work place. Put them into context and use them. It is all acquired knowledge and reference material you can draw upon.

3.8. Inspire by thought

As a sports coach, people may expect you to constantly be innovative or different in the methods you employ. The more innovative you are, the more likely you are to be memorable and the more that sticks when all of the action is happening; the more chance you and your star has of success.

I have heard many tales of different coaching styles and techniques in sport. Usually these involved equipment of some kind or the use of alternative and contrasting activity. For example, I knew of a Pub Team football coach who had his players attempting gymnastics and another who wouldn't let them train with a ball, the idea being that they would be hungry for the ball come match day. I believe there are two things for which there are no substitutes in sports coaching and these elements can be carried across to business coaching. Practice what it is you are going to be doing, i.e. if you are a swimmer, swim; a golfer should play golf and so on. The second thing is to encourage thinking and not just straight line thinking, encourage lateral thinking. A sports person may have to adapt, during the course of an event, dependent upon the competition, the conditions, how they are playing that day and so on.

In business, those two elements should also be fundamental to your approach. There is little point starting to plan a technical Communications cabinet build if your key function is Project Management. Similarly, think constantly about the job and the way it is going. Look at progress and, if it is not going well, think about a different approach and how that might affect what it is you are doing.

People tend to think in straight lines and follow processes which are established. That is not a bad thing, if it produces the outcome you want every time. In sport, you can be too formulaic as a coach, and the opposition will spot that and counter it. That's when it all starts to unravel, unless you have an alternative. Sometimes, it is about the genius of the individual, or a team player, who will change it around on the spot and wrong foot the opponents.

In business scenarios, you are not always pitted against other thinking, breathing organisms. Sometimes it is objects and established ways of doing things which can cause you potential problems. It is for just such circumstances that you need to coach the ability to think outside of the box.

That may sound simple, but it relies on a couple of fundamental premises. You and those you are coaching must know their business or sport in detail, not only that, they need to be able to construct and deconstruct, what it is they do, effortlessly.

I can relate a couple of actual scenarios here that I heard about, which are classic examples of that kind of thinking; one from sport and one from business.

In the business example, a Store Operator had a temporary Store trading from Portakabins, whilst the main Store was being rebuilt after a fire. Having traded for several months from the temporary outlet, the time came for the rebuilt unit to become operational, if not necessarily trading. There was though, a problem with that. In order to commence any sort of business, including drawing of stock, setting up Store specific systems and even training on EPOS systems, the re-built Store needed a Store number and the temporary Store was already using it. The creation of a new Store number, even for a short period, would have caused issues, but without it many financial and operational processes could not be initiated.

A meeting was called with all the Central specialists, I.T. people and business process specialists, who scratched their heads, wondering how to handle the problem. All seemed to be lost, when one of the group, a semi-technical, but well experienced individual suggested that the back office of the new Store became the back office for both units and the EPOS be split so that the first eight EPOS units were the eight in the temporary unit and the first EPOS unit active in the rebuilt Store would be number nine. This would continue until the rebuilt Store opened for trading, when the first eight would then become active and the temporary unit would close. From an ordering and accounting perspective, both units would operate as if they were one Store. The solution was simple, elegant, but what made it particularly special was that it didn't conform to the straight lines and processes that were already established. No solution that occupied those spaces would have worked because the situation was unique. The person who came up with the solution simply looked at what the end game needed to be and assessed potential options. He didn't take account of accepted conventions and processes, but he did use his knowledge of the art of the possible. This is what effectively won the day. Look at what you want to achieve; what the goal is and don't discount anything straight away. If you do, a good possible solution could be discarded early on. In this example, the best business coach he had worked with had suggested just that.

In the sporting example consider the example set by Richard Noble. In his pursuit of breaking the land speed record, Richard threw aside the convention that any potential land speed record breaking attempt should be approached in the same way as before; i.e. a car. Effectively, being an aviator and a designer, he designed a road going jet plane, the biggest challenge being to keep the vehicle on the ground. Subsequent designs have all followed Nobles template, rather than the legacy rocket car templates of such pioneers as Donald Campbell.

In your coaching and in your work, you must try and keep it fresh and inspire thought. Don't set boundaries which will restrict a colleague or a player. As long as they are operating legally, within the rules or laws which should be observed, any solution or idea can be explored.

A true milestone in you developing someone, with your coaching, is when they feel both confident enough and knowledgeable enough to think about their own coaching points and even come up with more radical and different mechanisms to help them improve. I maintain that a lot of these will surface when you have seen consistent levels of achievement in one area. People will generally enjoy the experience of doing a good job and to make the connection between their coaching and that achievement will be one of the defining moments for them in the process.

If you would like to explore more about encouraging thinking, particularly innovative or team based thinking, you might like to explore the 'Six Thinking Hats' principle as described by Edward De Bono.

The thinking hats concept is one where each 'hat' represents a mode of thinking and where, wearing one hat, you should avoid thinking in other modes. This separates types of thinking and allows the individuals or groups to focus more on particular elements. I'm not advocating that you structure 'thinking sessions' but encourage your people to focus their thinking and not to confuse different types of thinking.

The white hat
The white hat is all about what you know and what you need. It should be factual and actual; figures, facts, data. The thinking should allow these to be presented in an objective manner without any emotion or pre-conceived ideas. The focus should be just on the information you have and what else is available or you may need. If there are elements you don't have, you might consider how you would obtain them and in what format. With this hat on, any arguments, disagreements or beliefs have no place. So, simply:
What information do we have here?
What information is missing?
What information would we like to have?
How are we going to get the information?

The yellow hat
This hat is about the art of the possible and the 'glass is half full' approach. It calls for a logical and positive view seeking out the feasibility without getting hung up on the difficulties. The main focus is on the benefits of doing something and how we might achieve it. It is also about taking creativity to another level and making it come alive. Questions you may ask in the thought process are:

What are the benefits of this option?
Why is this proposal preferable?
What are the positive assets of this design?
How can we make this work?

The black hat

As you might expect the black hat is about judgement, caution and evaluation. This is where you might analyse an idea or proposal critically and determine why it just doesn't seem to sit right. You might consider such areas as cost, does it look to expensive; too cheap? Does it not really stack up? You might consider legislation or regulations; is the suggestion likely to fall foul of either of those or indeed, the law? Is it practical? It may be a good aesthetic design but will it actually work? What about the consistency of it? Would it be costly to maintain or need frequent maintenance? The black hat will help you look at all the areas where you should be cautious and most critical, but take care not to kill off a great idea with too much negativity. This is about what might go wrong or not work. It may be that having been given the black hat treatment, an idea passed to another hat (another way of thinking) could be improved and adopted.

The red hat

There is a lot to be said for the way experienced people can usually spot a lemon. It doesn't have to be about hard evidence or statistics, it can just be a feeling. The red hat allows you to exercise your intuition, without having to justify it with explanations or hard facts. It might be as simple as you don't feel comfortable with the proposal or idea. It might be the way in which it is being approached. You might not believe that it will work or address the issues it is supposed to. You should coach and encourage people to use their experience in this way and to exercise their views like this. Sometimes, in doing so, you will get a lot of the emotion behind a piece of work out into the open and be able to deal with it there and then. This will help smooth the way later.

The green hat

If you want to be creative and innovative, wear the green hat. It is to encourage creative thinking, alternatives, discussing the art of the possible and hypothesising. It may be what some call 'blue sky thinking', although with a green hat. It is difficult to do because it flies in the face of our present knowledge, judgement and our critical nature. Sometimes the green hat will mean putting aside convention and looking for different ways of doing things and exploring ideas which might be a little off the wall. You should encourage it, because sometimes the best ideas come from the most bizarre angles. Without them we would not have the camera, telephone, airplane etc.

The blue hat

This hat controls the thinking so that it is organised and structured and therefore more productive. It might be that you use this to set an agenda, lay out the next steps or just come up with a format so that the various stages or components of the objective or project are separated and thought about in different ways; perhaps using one of the other 'hats'. The product of this kind of thinking is therefore not concerned with an idea, innovation or revelation, but with a clear plan on how you might think through and get to one of those things. Think about a steering group. This is what a steering group should primarily be about. Not the detailed thinking, but the way in which the thinking should be done and the direction it should ultimately take.

Having looked at the 'hats' and what they are all about, you may wonder where they have a place in sport and the thinking behind sport coaching? It is relatively easy to align each of them to a sport context.
White – Statistics, facts; what do we know about the opponent?
Yellow – Examining the approach, will it work, is it a good strategy?
Black – What might go wrong, do we need to think through an alternative?
Red – Gut feel, instinct, important in sport once you have left the blocks.

Green – Dream a little, what is it going to be like to be out front, how do we handle that?

Blue – Organise the other thoughts into a sequence, use the product of the others in a logical and structured way.

3.8. Moving them on

In my days as a Swimming coach, one of the hardest things to do, was to pass the developing swimmers onwards and upwards to the next group. Strange though it may seem, that was the ultimate goal we had as coaches of that group. We developed and coached the children to a level where they were ready for the next phase of their journey. In the next group, they would train more hours per week, they would be introduced to more rigorous and challenging repetitions and they would start to compete at a national level.

It didn't make it any easier though. The swimmers concerned had joined the group with some ability, often limited, had been coached and taught the correct technique, had been nurtured and corrected, motivated and developed. Being able to see someone go through that transition and know that you have played a massive part in it is a very satisfying thing, but then you have to let go.

If you don't, or you let them linger too long, you will affect their future development. They might start to become bored, because they are no longer challenged or they might lose ground on others of a similar age and skill who are moved up. Timing is quite often the most important key.

In business too, you should not only be prepared to let someone move onwards and upwards, you should positively encourage it. Not only that, if you can provide an environment where there is the opportunity and the structure to allow it to happen, then you will still benefit as an organisation.

Too many businesses and the departmental structures created within them don't offer those opportunities. In fact, the managers and team leaders would rather not lose someone they have spent months or years developing, because they will have to start the process all over again. Well, what do I say to that? Tough; Sports coaches do it all the time and they not only enjoy it, they see it as a positive. It is a testament to their ability to coach, develop and prepare their charges for the next step.

In business, we really need to get a grip and embrace that sort of thinking. If a talented individual with bags of potential has to leave your organisation, because there are no perceived opportunities for them to progress further, you have failed. Many firms are beginning to take this on board and develop more skill based structures. They will deliberately teach and coach people on transferable skills, having first identified each of these, in each role, at each level. This is not an easy task, but it is well worth doing if you want to take full advantage of the investment you have made in your people.

It also touches upon something that is a rather important and often neglected consideration. If someone has a skill in sport, it may be transferable to another sport, where they can achieve more. In business, if we know what the required skills are for a role we can begin to match the skills to the people to enable them to develop their careers. They don't have to follow one single path. They can, in effect, become professional managers.

Let's look at an example.

An administrator, in a specialist technology team, raises orders for components on behalf of the technical specialists and engineers. They ensure that these items are procured in a timely manner, arrive where they should and are purchased at the right price. They also monitor expenditure for each of the teams they service and produce reports on what and where the expenditure is being made. So what skills do they need to do this?

- They need administrative skills.
- They need to be able to work to schedules and deadlines.
- They need to be negotiators.

- They need to keep accurate records, based on hard fact.
- They can assimilate technical data to an acceptable level of understanding.
- They produce timely reports.
- They need to be able to use appropriate software.

With these particular skills and some input they could become a Project Co-ordinator or even a Project Manager. So when they reach that point in their development where the Administrator job looks too easy and they seem like they need a challenge, you might look towards Project Management as a potential avenue for them to explore. It might be that you give them a Project to co-ordinate just to test the water. With appropriate input and coaching, they should handle it without any issues. It is this sort of forward thinking which will help keep people in your business and keep them challenged. I don't think that we do enough in business generally, to let people know what avenues are open to them and that their career need not follow a straight line. Of course this is just one example and a fairly simple one. Once you start to compare common skills across the spectrum of your job roles, you will see the potential.

In sport, it should be a whole lot easier. If you are a decent runner, either fast or enduring, there are many sports where this could be an advantage. It is a core skill and very transferrable. If you have good hand to eye co-ordination, the same applies. The difference between business and sport is that in sport, it is mainly pretty obvious. In business the skills people have are not generally on display as they execute their tasks. It is sometimes only when you see the results that you realise how talented they might be.

There is a great quote from Darwin on this subject;

"It is not the strongest of the species that survive nor the most intelligent, but the one most responsive to change."

If you think about it, this is also true in sport and business. The sports people with longevity are ones who adapt their game, or even change sports as they get older and their physiology changes. In business, quite often, those who stay at a firm the longest have changed roles several times and been responsive to changes in the way things are done and changes in the business, with the least fuss. It would be prudent, I believe, to bear this in mind when you are coaching. Don't think of yourself or your charges as an entity you are creating, with a defined and fixed scope. The team might have a relatively fixed brief and shape to it, but the individuals need to be able to adapt and grow. You may think that this conflicts with the theme of this and the previous chapter, where I advocated turning the shape to a sculpture and the sculpture to a masterpiece. The best sculptures are not necessarily those which are figurative, but those with no discernible point of reference or inspiration. They are the ones where your interpretation and imagination are used to full effect to appreciate the piece.

One final point to make, which I recall from my Swimming coaching days, is that those children who went on to higher groups, including the National Squad, never forgot the input they had from us. They quite often came back to tell us how they were doing and shared their success. When was the last time that happened to you in business?

In this chapter, we have taken our whole approach a stage further and become almost scientific. We have looked back right to the very start of the process, like a sports scout would, when we are interviewing and recognising talent. What is it we are looking for, those key elements that will give us a great foundation to work from? We have then looked at how we develop talent, and how we assess those we are working with, using the talent matrix, the skills matrix and T.A.S.K analysis. We have discussed inspiring people by our own example and that of others and also by thought. Getting people to think the right things at the right time is one of the keys to driving inspiration. We have looked at different ways of thinking and how by disseminating the different types of thought process we can focus them in the way they approach a particular piece of work or an issue. Finally we looked at the hardest of all stages of development; letting go. When we have done all that *we* can and brought them to a point where we need to move them on.

In chapter four we look in detail at the science we use in the art of coaching and how rules and theories are repeatable and solid, but are delivered in a flowing and interesting style.

CHAPTER 4.
THE SCIENCE IN THE ART OF COACHING

I could argue that science and art are a part of the same thing. They define each other and are probably more closely aligned than those who think of themselves as scientists or artists would care to believe. In this chapter and the next we will explore first coaching from a scientific viewpoint and then from an artistic one.

Before we go any further though, let's just think about 'science'. What is it? Science is a way of defining something with a set of rules and theories which are demonstrable, repeatable and consistent. If we talk about coaching as an art and we want to look at the science in it, we are essentially looking at the defining principles which make it repeatable and consistent.

Think about an artist, mixing paint. They are using an artistic eye, but using the science of mixing colours and pigments. A potter, turning a pot on a wheel is using science in the technique, the speed the wheel turns and the texture of the clay he or she is turning; then there is geometry, a science which art would be lost without. Have I made my point?

So what are we talking about in terms of sport and business; art and science? There is quite clearly a science in coaching sport. It is demonstrable, repeatable and consistent. It uses scientific techniques in the approach. In business, the same must apply. Otherwise how would we ever develop anyone? We would have to redefine the basic principles every single time.

Now you might say, *'Fine, I accept that science is used in coaching, but what about the art?'* As we will explore, art is about interpretation, proportion and representation. As a coach you will take the science of the subject matter and apply those three tenets to it. You will do it without thinking, because it just seems the right way. Once you have read this chapter, you will understand a little more of what we are trying to achieve and you will begin to think consciously about your interpretation and representation of coaching points and at the same time keep things in proportion.

4.1. Don't de-motivate

Whilst motivation is a relatively easy thing to achieve, whether it is through positive feedback, rewards, promotion or even just a simple gesture, de-motivation is something which, by and large, is ignored. There are many more things that can de-motivate, than there are those which motivate. This is because motivation tends to be personal, to an individual, but de-motivation can affect the whole team, group or department.

In sport, a team may be de-motivated by another teams results; a badly worded comment by their coach or manager, off the field business happening at the club, and any number of other things. Let's not forget either that, as a team, you are only as effective as the weakest member at any particular time. It only takes one or two members of the team to have an off day, and the whole performance will be below standard. You can, of course, make changes. In business, it is far less easy to make in flight substitutions, than it is in a game.

I have also seen examples in business where continual external appointments, rather than internal promotions can de-motivate the whole team, rather than just those who might have believed they had a chance. After a time, this will engender the belief that you will always go outside for higher level people and those already there will be bypassed. They will be de-motivated, switch off; possibly leave. Is it not far better to improve your development regime and your coaching, so that you can promote from within?

Sport recognised this many years ago and started to build academies so that they could develop and nurture their own talent. The good ones are real success stories as they are continually either bringing young players through into the reserve teams then the first team, or are feeding other clubs and making money out of the transfers.

A similar process in business, whilst not easy or cheap to set up, will end up paying dividends. An academy approach will give people a clear development path, a curriculum of training and definite goals to aim for in personal development. It shows that the business is keen to keep you and build you into the kind of employee or manager it will need going forward and it allows you to assess capabilities against a framework that is measurable

What else de-motivates? Lack of rewards, lack of opportunities, other people not pulling their weight and not being challenged about it, bad processes or worse, no processes, the behaviours of others and a whole host of things. They can all occur in sport and in business and they can all be addressed by good quality coaching. There is a simple key to coaching and it applies more closely to not de-motivating, than any other aspect of coaching. The key is timing. You should always look for the de-motivating factors and deal with them in a timely manner; most of the time, in most instances, that will be immediately. You can quite easily say to someone, in a motivational way, 'You're really doing well at the moment, these last few weeks have been great, keep it up,' and it's still relevant and positive and it works. It is absolutely no use at all to say 'I've been watching you these last few weeks and you've not been firing on all cylinders, what's wrong?' This approach would be much, much too late.

Similarly, language like; 'I don't think...' and 'You shouldn't...' Will put them on the defensive and load all the responsibility back on to them. Instead, take some of the blame yourself and involve yourself in the issues, 'What if we try....' and 'maybe we could...' are much more likely to affect a response.

Lack of rewards is an easy one to neglect. Especially in challenging economic climates, it is difficult to give people the financial rewards they might believe they deserve. Lack of opportunity though is just abuse. You should always make sure there are opportunities for people to stretch themselves, do something rewarding or go for a promotion or elevation.

You should also consider the difference between being a Coach and Critic. A critic may say good things and bad things in equal measure, but these comments or criticisms have no purpose other than to highlight the good and bad things. On their own, they are just statements, based upon observations, which anyone could make. A coach will look beyond that. They will still see the bad things, the negatives, but look at what positive opportunities they present. They will see the good things and know where even they need to be developed. As we said earlier, the sculpture is chipped at, taking it all forward as a whole, not one part before the other. This enables a controlled and smooth improvement, over time, rather than what would appear to be disproportionate focus or improvement.

In a sports team or a business department, those who seem to be getting away with not pulling their weight will de-motivate others. They will feel that they are carrying that person, they will feel resentment, they will discuss that person amongst themselves and concur that, if it was they who were behaving like that, they would be dealt with straight away. If you are aware of a member of the team letting the side down, you must deal with it. The first step is to find out why. Are they lazy? Do they have personal problems? Are they not up to the task? Whatever the reason, as a coach, you must find that out first and then deal with it accordingly. It is not as simple as saying *'Hey, you're not pulling your weight, snap out of it and sort yourself out.'* If it was that simple, people would be doing it all the time. It is about dealing with the issue, head on, but with some sensitivity. If given the right trigger question, most people will take the opportunity to open up. You are probably, therefore, wondering how that relates to coaching.

I had a member of staff in my team who would have the odd day off sick, on a pretty frequent basis. It may have been a day here a day there, amounting to about three days per month and, whilst not a big problem to begin with, became a pattern, which I and others noticed. I brought the subject up one day, in a sort of 'one to one' meeting. I asked if the health issues were related to one another and if there was some underlying medical condition I should be aware of. The answer was no, so I probed further. I asked if it was the work getting them down; the job they were doing. There was a pause, before a very unconvincing "No" again. I suggested a change of roles, as it happened we had a project coming up that needed someone with their particular skill set and I punted the idea that they might like to take a secondment to it. There was an immediate change in the body language and expression. They opened up and told me how the job they were doing was not challenging and how they felt trapped. They told me how they had seen others change roles and felt jealous. A salutary lesson to me not to take people for granted in roles. Just because they look comfortable, doesn't mean they are. I moved them onto the project and divided their work up amongst the others in the team. They never threw an odd sick day again.

When I was working on the large project I have mentioned a couple of times already, the guys out in the field who were executing my plan, would gather each Friday for a de-briefing with their line manager. The de-briefing would include a report, from them, on their experiences through the week, which they would share with the team. Some of the incidents, discoveries and solutions would be common, as the ultimate goal was always the same and the infrastructure similar. Their shared input would be helpful to the others if they hadn't encountered those particular circumstances yet. The de-briefing, particularly where issues were concerned, was not about recriminations or blame. It was a collective learning and coaching experience. There was no time, no slack in our programme for a blame culture or to make someone feel that they were responsible for a failure. Instead, we just moved on and made sure we hit the target. The catchphrase most often used was, 'We are where we are.' This particular statement was an appropriate message. Wherever you find yourself, if you need to put something right, the primary concern should be to get on and deal with it, not waste a lot of time analysing how you got there.

You should always ask yourself how you would feel, or how you would think if you were given feedback or experienced behaviour which de-motivated you. You probably already have examples of your own; use them to avoid doing the same to your teams. Involve them in the feedback by saying things like *'What if we try....'* or *'Maybe we could....'* rather than *'You shouldn't....* or *'I don't think...'* Your opinion, however valid if coached in those terms will de-motivate. Keep the feeling of a partnership between coach and coachee alive.

4.2. Sandwich or Pizza?

There are many schools of thought about the way in which you should deliver critique. As in the previous section, negative comments can demotivate, but sometimes they are necessary and need to be aired. You can't go on believing that everything can be turned into a positive. A footballer with a bad temperament, sent off in several games for punching a member of the other team, cannot possibly be regarded in any other way than negatively, unless his pugilistic skills are so good that it could lead to a change of career!

Some advocate a sort of news sandwich. That is to say a good – bad – good message. The idea here is to give them a positive lead in, followed by the negative critique, and closed with a positive element. The thinking behind it is that the target will take away two positive remarks and only one negative one. An example in sport might be, to our Golfer, *'Great swing, good contact, slightly off line though, you could have been further left, try making the shot draw a little next time, but excellent length, you should have a neat chip from there.'* You see the sandwich effect? The first part is related to the third part, but they have been split, the negative coaching point here is about where the ball ended up and how to make the ball draw left next time. It is almost lost in the enthusiastic revelling in the contact and distance of the hit.

In business, this can also be true. A member of the team has just presented a pack of slides. The presentation was lack lustre, but the content of the slides and the slide pack, quite good. Here we could tell them that the slides were great, informative and clear. You could say then that they could have picked out a few key elements and made more of them, spiced them up a bit; been a bit more dynamic. Then close the piece off by saying that the structure and format was really good and that they should use that again.

So what have you done? You have told them they were not very good at presenting. It didn't come across that way. With the golfer, he could still be saying to himself, *'But I have a neat chip to the green.'* It can be a bit weak and the sandwich effect will become rather clichéd after a while. You will want to give him the negative comments, but feel obliged to come up with two slices of bread to wrap the meat in. When that moment arrives; and you struggle to find the bread, that's when the whole deal falls down.

So should it be more of a Pizza? Open, all the elements on display and colourful?

A lot depends on the relationship you forge as a coach with your team. If you have to dress a criticism up with two positive comments either side you do not really have the kind of relationship you should have with your charges. Consider this. I give or offer someone a sandwich. What is the first question they are likely to ask? What's in it? They don't bite it and say, 'Oh good, chicken.' They ask first. Give them or offer them a slice of Pizza and they will almost certainly recognise the elements on it straight away.

In my view, the relationship you should develop, in order to be able to deliver this kind of critique is one where you can show them the pizza. So they can see for themselves what is on it and recognise both the good and the bad points.

Let's go back to the golfer. He's hit the shot, it's too far right. Here's what we do. *'Okay, not bad distance there, what do you think to the position?'* Now you have him thinking. If he doesn't come up with the right answer, you could follow up with, *'Do you think if you had gone a bit further left, it would have given you a better line to the green?'* Again, you will have him thinking and you can offer the point, to try a bit of a draw next time to bring the ball further left.

In our business context it's much the same approach. *'Good slides, how do you think it went, do you think you emphasised the key points?'* If they recognise that they were a bit one paced and flat, great. If not you can follow up with your view that certain points could have been reinforced with a stronger delivery. Perhaps you could even demonstrate it to them? You could even get them to ask the audience at the presentation for feedback on the 'key points'. This will demonstrate to them, whether they have put it across well or not.

People are generally not stupid. They will appreciate the honesty and forthright approach, as long as it is done with sensitivity. They will quickly see through the sandwich approach as a bit of subterfuge. Forget the psychobabble about how negative feedback should always be avoided as it de-motivates, it is all about the relationship and how it is approached.

There is a further view, that you should only give one negative element of feedback for every seven positives. The balance there seems like overkill to me and you may struggle to come up with seven positives all the time. Instead of wasting time thinking about these positives and dressing up all the negatives, work on the relationship. The stronger that is, the easier it is to be absolutely honest and, whilst not necessarily negative in your critique, more open.

4.3. What makes a good Coach?

I will attempt to articulate what makes a *good* coach, without giving the game away for the next section on what makes a *great* coach. It may not be that easy.

A good coach will get the best out of *you*. It is that simple. Remember the key difference between teaching and coaching *'Teach in, Coach out'*. We should not forget either, the other 'T' word that falls somewhere between the two; Training. Training is a form of teaching, incorporating some coaching. At its most effective, training is done at the same time, so that coaching points can be added into repetitive training sessions.

So aside from the throw-away line above 'A good coach will get the best out of *you*.' What can we say to make this a whole lot more interesting and easier to digest?

There are a number of points to consider here. There are many good coaches, in all walks of life, business and sports. They all have a number of things in common. They are people focussed first and experts in what they do second.

Why is that important? Why are the most eminent and experienced people, in a particular field, not necessarily the best coaches? It is an interesting question. Let me answer it like this; as a good coach, I could, with the smallest amount of exposure to the subject matter, coach anyone in anything. Coaching isn't necessarily about the subject matter per-se, but the attitude and approach to it. This applies in sport equally as it applies in business.

A good coach will analyse the main operation, whether it is a business one or a sporting one and break it down into components. Whether they do it consciously or not, that is what they do. They will then look at the performance of the team or an individual and examine how they operate around those elements, before coming up with a coaching point or two, to improve how things are being done. Let's look at a couple of examples.

I had a friend who had never seen a competitive track race before, other than on the TV. He was amazed how a 1500 metre runner, who came in third, by about 10 metres, seemed to be the only one who was not out of breath at the finish. He commented, *'He wasn't working hard enough. If he had all that left, but not a great finishing pace, why didn't he go earlier?'*

A good point well made. The runner had energy left in the tank, but had not planned his strategy, with his coach, to match his abilities. Or perhaps he had, but had just not executed it properly. It was being close to the runners at the finish which showed us what sort of condition the guys were in and enabled him to make that comment. He was not a running coach, he was not even that athletic himself, but he could see that something hadn't gone quite as it should. You probably wouldn't pick that up on TV, unless the pundits spotted it. I daresay that my friend could have gone to the runner and said something about going earlier and stretching the field out and that would have paid dividends. As I said, the point was obvious and probably valid. The coach in this case clearly worked on the runner's strategy, as the next time we saw him, he went for it on lap three, before the bell and took the others by surprise, winning by a good 20 metres himself. All it probably took was getting him to look more closely at the field and ask himself a few questions; *Are there fast finishers here? Are there runners like me who can go earlier, but not as fast?* He could then translate that data into a strategy.

From business, I have a similar example. I once worked with a chap who had good organisational and operational skills and great technique in performing aspects of manual work. He was promoted to Manager of a department where these skills were fundamental to the operation, because his coach (Manager) believed that this was the best logical step. He failed, because his man management skills were under-developed, his approach to people as a 'boss' were, quite weak and he lacked some credibility in aspects of his private life which had spilled over into his working life. For about ten months he struggled to emulate the success he had previously enjoyed and to enable his team to be as good as he was. Luckily for him a better coach (Manager) came along. This manager, after a very short time, recognised his true strengths and skills and where his weak areas would not be so evident. He was recommended for a Regional Training role, teaching the very skills in which he excelled. He executed this by showing people exactly how it should be done and explaining his thinking behind it. Result. The new manager did not know in immense detail how to organise and operate the areas our man did, but could see that he was a square peg trying to fit in a round hole.

In short, a good coach will recognise a person or team's strengths and attempt to exorcise its weaknesses.

You should also consider what sort of coach you are going to be. This will be dependent upon the session, and the message you want to get across. Do you need to be friendly or adversarial? Do you need to be compassionate or aggressive? Mix it up. Don't always be the same.

A good sports coach will always have in mind that their charge or charges will be potential superstars. They are the reason they are coaching. They have the potential to achieve the goals and the glory. Whilst the coach is necessary to that process, they may not necessarily be indispensable.

In business it is a little different at first glance. Generally, those whom you are coaching are subordinates, which will mean that you are trying to get a good performance out of them in a given role or on a particular piece of work. You are coaching them primarily for their benefit, but ultimately, their success will benefit you. There is no greater achievement as a coach in business, to have one of your team promoted, through your input, your expertise as a coach and their talent, ability to engage with you and adopt your guidance.

A good relationship or rapport will mean that you can have a joke with them. It will mean that you can tell them openly and plainly any truth about their approach, performance or limitations. As a coach, although some conversations are difficult, you should not fear them or put them off. You should only be mindful of how you execute them.

A good coach will use analogies to get the message across. Especially if the concept they are trying to get across deals with a scientific process or has its roots in psychology. When I coached swimming, I used to try and get the message about the movement of the water across by using the analogy of marbles. If you imagined the pool was made up of marbles, once you had them moving, the less effect a steady pull would have. Even the younger kids could see and understand that. In business it might not always be so easy to come up with an analogy, but your supporting narrative may also be anecdotal. There is absolutely nothing wrong with a story which illustrates the point, which may have nothing to do with business. In fact, this is exactly where this book and concept has its foundation.

A good coach will always try and simplify. You have to break everything down and reconstruct it. This is the only way that a person will properly understand and respond to what you are asking them to do. It can also be true of an individual. In a Swimming stroke or a Golf swing you can break the whole thing down into sections or stages and describe each one and its purpose. Importantly, a good coach will explain how that component contributes to the whole thing.

A good coach will have energy and enthusiasm. You can't coach from a platform of apathy. If you don't have the energy and enthusiasm for what you are doing or saying, how do you expect that to be carried across to those you are coaching? This is where, sometimes, a little bit of role playing can pay dividends. Even coaches have days when they feel less than 100% and unless you want that to be passed on to your team you need to be able to switch on the 'good coach' button when you hit the playing turf.

A good coach will be supportive. It is always easier to be critical in a destructive way, because as a coach, to achieve the best outcomes, you will be looking for the things you need to improve. A good coach will also be looking for the things which support the individual, or the team. You can't bash them with the bad stuff. It has to be on the lines of *'That was good but you might try……'* and suggest an improvement. Better still, get them to suggest it.

There are, in addition, a number of other things a good coach will do or should develop as a matter of course. Some of them you may do already, but they are taken from the point of view of a sports coach and modified slightly, so don't be discouraged if you're not. Think of them in relation to your own environment and adapt them accordingly.

A good coach will establish a relationship with the members of the team, or the individual, which will be as close and as open as it needs to be to achieve the best results. Many sports coaches live and breathe the lives of their individual charges, advising on and monitoring things like diet, rest, public exposure etcetera. In business that might not be quite as possible or necessary. It is however, a good point at which to consider another sport/business comparison.

Always coach on things you have seen for yourself. Don't rely upon or act upon something someone else has pointed out to you. They are not as close to the individual or team and the plan you have in place for development. They may not interpret what they have seen in the same way. You will also lose credibility if you start by saying something like *'I was talking to John and he said he'd seen you…….'* You're the coach. You need to work with your own observations.

A good coach will also be a good salesperson. You need to sell your ideas and your coaching points to the individual. Sometimes that might mean explaining the dynamics of an improvement or how something might play out. You are a partner to their vision, objectives; their challenges and in developing their skills. They need to be 100% sold on the coaching you are giving them and the plan you have in place. You must always remember that people have their own ideas and, whilst they might not always be the same as yours, should be taken into account and if appropriate, factored into the coaching.

Coaching is also about being clear and concise. As we said earlier, you must try and get across your points in a manner they will digest easily. If that means breaking it down, then do so and don't immediately blame them if they get it wrong. I attended an intense Communications and Networks Seminar in the late eighties, chaired by Dr Donald Haring. The good doctor was an American who had worked on such projects as the Apollo missions and certainly knew his subject. When questions were asked about a particular theme he had just been explaining, he would start by saying, *'Guess I did a good job there right?'* He would blame himself, immediately, for the lack of understanding, not think that the person asking the question was at fault, or hadn't listened.

A good coach will consider the position or stance they adopt whilst coaching. They will never, for example, coach across a desk as this creates a barrier. They will not coach if they feeling angry or upset or if the person they are coaching is similarly out of sorts. The art in the science here is to coach when conditions are right. If you try and coach someone when you are not ready for it, or they are pre-occupied, then you are really wasting each other's time.

A good coach will look to build upon a person's strengths and not always focus upon their weak areas. We said in an earlier chapter that people will tend to focus on elements of a project that are going well and avoid or ignore the parts that are not going so well, and that you should coach them otherwise. In coaching an individual and their attributes you should consider that improving what they are already good at, might be a better way of improving something they are not so good at. If we consider sport again for a moment, you might have a Swimmer whose turns are brilliant, but their underwater technique is not so good. You would coach them to focus on getting more power out of those brilliant turns, in an effort to improve the underwater speed, rather than focussing primarily on improving the underwater technique. Similarly, a Golfers tee shots may be so accurate and well struck, that he can get a great fairway position most times, and his big fairway shots are equally good, but his short play is suspect. You might encourage him to hit a shorter, more accurately placed drive, so that his longer second shot comes into play, rather than a short chip, which he may not be so successful with. It is, I guess, a bit of a trade off.

One other thing that a good coach may do is to set an example. In sport this is perhaps not as easy as it is in business, given that you are most likely to be coaching a sportsperson who is more skilled, or potentially more talented than you. However there are still disciplines that are common. Punctuality is one key area. Be on time for work or for coaching sessions, be correctly and properly attired for the work you are doing. Have the right equipment and ensure it works. Always be courteous and respectful of the person you are coaching and consider, *'how would I want to be treated?'* In business, where you are probably executing a lot more of the elements you are coaching on yourself anyway, you must always practice what you are preaching. There is little point in spending time passing on these hints and tips to an individual, or a team, if you don't stand by them yourself. They will be looking for them in you, of that you should have no doubt.

One final point and one we will take forward. One undeniable trait of any good coach; they are all good listeners.

4.4. What makes a great Coach?

So, what makes a great coach? In a nutshell a great coach helps you get the best out of yourself. As you might imagine though, there is much more to it than that. You can take all of the things we discussed in the previous section and amplify them then, add in a good deal more.

Being a great coach is not something just anyone can be. In the same way that not every Golfer or Tennis player will win a major, it is that extra something that will define whether we are good (sometimes very good) or great.

Most people being coached will not have as high expectations of themselves, as you might have, as their coach. You have the benefit of recognising their talent and potential, knowing the plan and being a great coach, you know it will all come together. You must try and communicate that to them so that they believe it and have faith in their own abilities. Once you do that, you have worked them through quite a difficult barrier. The job then is all about proving it to them. If you can show them tangible evidence that the coaching you have given and the talent they have is achieving those results, the whole process will become so much easier going forwards.

I'm not promising that by reading this you will become a great coach, but if you become a good coach, these additional tips and thoughts will take you that bit further. It might be that what ultimately makes you a great coach is down to the inherent quality of those you end up coaching. As I said to a group of parents once, who complemented me on the work I had done with their children, *'I can only work with who comes in through the door.'*

Great coaches, from what I have observed, in both sport and business, don't just look at the business or sport the person being coached is engaged in and how they approach it, they look at the person. Now I know in the earlier section I said good coaches were people focussed first, but there is a difference. It all depends upon where you are prepared to position yourself as a coach. I don't mean physically, but importantly, in the eyes of the people you are coaching, what space do they think you occupy? What space are you prepared to occupy?

It might seem obvious. *'I am the coach. You are learning and improving based on my observations and input. I am therefore the key to your plans.'* Cue the noise the computer makes when you get the answer wrong! A great coach will not look at the individual in those terms; they will elevate the status of the individual or the team and ensure that they were in no doubt how important they were to the coach and/or the coaching team.

There are other fundamentals that separate out a great coach. A great coach is not afraid of failure, or admitting failure. They are not afraid of being wrong, neither are they afraid of admitting to their infallibilities. All of these things can be used as teaching and coaching points.

At the very end of the previous section we discussed listening. It is fair to say that a great coach will not just listen to what is said they will also listen to the silences; those things which are not said. These will be facial expressions, the body language and positioning of the hands and general posture of the person being coached. These signals are to be read and interpreted and then acted upon. A mark of a great coach is not putting off saying or dealing with something, which needs dealing with. Procrastination can be destructive.

When a great coach is talking they will use the expression 'I' and not 'you', which is a great way of demonstrating where the accountability lies. To give an example, if you were coaching a member of staff how to approach a difficult task, you might say *'What I would do is…..'*, rather than, *'What you need to do is……'* If the team or individual hears you say what you would do, it is a lot stronger than appearing to put all the responsibility and accountability on them.

The ultimate aim of the great coach is to deliver a programme that makes the individual or team feeling good about the coaching they have just had, but equally make them want to come back for more. They will only want to do this if they have felt like they have learned something or achieved something and have gone away feeling better than when they began that session. As a good coach, you will never be a great coach unless you master the art of turning negatives into positives and always try to make being coached feel like even their mistakes or failures have been glowing opportunities to learn. After all, how can you enjoy success for what it is, unless you have first tasted failure and defeat and are able to put them in their place; As Rudyard Kipling eloquently wrote, in his famous poem 'If'.

*"If you can meet with Triumph and Disaster
and treat those two impostors just the same:"*

They are indeed impostors. Without one, the other would not exist therefore they are synonymous and need each other. They enable us to measure one against the other, but in terms of being a measure they have no meaning. A failure or defeat is just as necessary as a triumph, in relation to the game, there has to be one for there to be another. Don't therefore discard or devalue one or the other. Treat them equally and ensure that whoever you are coaching does the same. I would be foolish to say that defeat or failure is a good thing, the reason we do what we do as coaches is to prevent those things, but let's not forget that winning all of the time can have some really bad side effects; complacency, expectation, a false sense of security. How many boxers can you recall who have gone through the first part of their professional career with a string of knockouts or stoppages, only to be shocked when they fight someone who can actually take a punch? Too many to be healthy I would wager. Unfortunately, the nature of that sport means that you have to work your way up the rankings and, as you do, you realise that the gulf between the competent and the very good is quite staggering.

In business, mistakes and failures are costly and in any climate that is unpopular. However, as a coach you can try to prevent actual failure if you see it about to happen and you can still use the exercise to coach the individuals concerned as to what would have happened and where they might have gone wrong. If someone does make a mistake, you should always analyse the mistake and see where they went wrong. It is RCA or root cause analysis. You, as a coach, should do this before you tackle the individual or team about it. The alternative is to steam in and the only outcome from that will be negative. Once you have determined the RCA, then you can decide how best to rectify the mistake and get them into a position where they can take a positive out of it. Let's be honest here, if you are accountable for them as members of your team, you are probably responsible for their mistake in the first place. A great coach will recognise this and will ensure that their charges know that this is the case. Remember, they are your most valuable asset and if you don't keep them aiming for the skies, they will end up in the dirt.

A great coach will take the root cause and come up with a plan to put things right, at the same time, they will not apportion blame, unless it is on themselves and they will turn the negative solidly into a positive experience.

Let me give you an example.

We had a job where two guys had to go to a site and co-ordinate the efforts of a few specialist suppliers – effectively trades – to complete a particular job. A programme of works had been completed, which showed all the dependencies and the sequence in which works should be executed. Up until a particular point, the guys had done a great job and followed the programme but then, at a critical point, one of the contractors had a road accident on the way to site and couldn't make it. Without consultation, and without wanting to delay the rest of the teams, they cracked on, believing that the works the unfortunate contractor was going to complete could be done later. What they hadn't considered was that to complete these works later, would undo some of the work already done and be quite disruptive. For disruptive, read costly. Their manager and 'coach' – yours truly – had set an expectation that they should be pragmatic and work their way around issues. That is just what they had done, not considering the implications. My first reaction when I found out was to think of a hundred ways I could rip them to pieces. My second thought was all about how I was going to explain it to my boss. My third thought was about another hundred ways I could rip them to pieces. I was, as you will have gathered, not a great coach. Not even a good coach at this stage.

Having calmed down and realised that their actions were in the best interests of the project, I tried to rationalise where they had made a mistake and – believe it or not – where I had gone wrong. I realised that there was no flexibility in the programme, for such occurrences, and that some of the dependencies were just too tight. Instead of bawling them out in the follow up meeting I took the blame squarely on the chin and we brainstormed the programme, looking for instances where one specialist or supplier not turning up or not hitting their deadline, would cause us a problem. At the end of a ninety minute session, we had re-engineered the programme and put contingencies in place, highlighted escalation points and clearly stated where unforeseen incidents meant that the responsibility and decision making was passed on from the guys on the ground. In future, none of the unfortunate occurrences would be repeated.

Now this is where I had learned something vital to my development as a coach. To be a great coach, you have to listen to those you are coaching and actually do what they want to do. In sport, as you may imagine, the coach is not out on the pitch, amidst the violent tackles, the inclement weather and all the other potential 'muck and bullets' which athletes will face. The coach watches from the side-lines, critical, but always thoroughly involved. There is a whole world of difference. Involved is not necessarily engaged. To be engaged, you have to be living it and feel the pain. You have to live those agonies with them. You have to experience their emotional journey. Those guys, from my team, felt the pain once they realised what their 'mistake' would mean. So how do you move forward from here? It is not that obvious, until it is mentioned. What I learned was that you can't always be remote from the thing you are coaching. As a swimming coach, I had to achieve a particular standard as a swimmer, in terms of speed and some aquatic skills, to be able to set foot on poolside, so why not in business? Once you have been out there and experienced the issues for yourself, you may be able to understand why they made the decision they made. Never underestimate the pressure that people may be under, which you may have created!

From this point a great coach will understand, what it is he needs to do to restore the status quo.

One final factor that will differentiate a good coach from a great coach is that a great coach will live their dream with them.

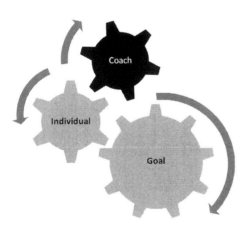

The coach is fundamental to the individual achieving their goal, as in the diagram they are a driving force, imparting direction and power. Ultimately the goal may be something the coach will help the individual to achieve by working towards it, even though the coaching, may not seem to reinforce it, or even appear to be at odds with it.

Many people don't understand the difference between being a mentor and a coach. They can actually be very close in terms of their definition, but generally the difference is that a coach will not necessarily be a former exponent in the area they are coaching; a mentor may have those skills. In that way, the mentor may be more likely to empathise with the coachee and understand many of the issues and problems that the coachee will face. This may, of course, also be true of the coach, but perhaps to a lesser degree. As a Swimming coach, and not being as talented as some of the people I was coaching, there were aspects I could not completely get my head around. Another swimmer though, who had gone through the same process could. We were fortunate that another coach we worked with had gone all the way through the scheme and right up to national level.

You may find that a good supplement to your coaching is to assign a mentor to a team member. It could be someone who perhaps is learning to be a coach, but who is also engaged in the same work/sport as the coachee. They will have that empathy and rapport and be able to help translate your coaching in 'real' terms. It is also a great way for you to get reliable feedback on your own coaching.

4.5. Team coaching

When you are coaching a team, you have to remember that people respond differently to the things we say. You could aim a coaching point at the whole team and it could be interpreted differently by each single member of the team.

In a sporting context, a football team manager might say, *'You all played well, in the first half, but in the second we just need to up the work rate a little and make sure those passes hit their targets.'* What's wrong with that? It wasn't negative. He didn't berate anyone for not working hard enough; he just indicated that everyone should pick it up a gear. He also reminded them to make their passes accurate, without singling anyone out. So what was actually wrong with it?

In the minds of the players, depending on how they perceived their own performance in the first half, they could interpret those comments quite differently. Those who felt they had worked hard would believe that the comment on work-rate was aimed at others, and they would be pretty sure they knew who that was. Those who had played a couple of duff passes could construe the comment about passing as a criticism of their particular contribution. The net result is that, some players would switch off, believing that the comments were not aimed at them, and others would take it personally.

Now some may take the attitude that, these are all big boys in a rough game and if they can't take a little criticism, they shouldn't be wearing the shirt. They are people, however and no matter how tough they are, they will react and respond to things that are said in the heat of the game. No-one said it was easy.

A better approach might have been to get members of the team to suggest what should be done in the second half. Those with any guilt about their work-rate would probably own up to it and say, we need to work harder. Those who have a hit a few stray passes may comment on more accuracy in passing. With those particular monkeys off their backs and out in the open, you can then build on it. You can point out to those who maybe haven't been firing on all cylinders that it would be a good thing and suggest how they might get more involved. To those whose passes have gone astray, you could encourage them to go for the easy option each time and not get too ambitious. If they are having an off day, best not to start trying to get them to hit 70 metre pinpoint passes.

In business it works just the same. Don't make generalisations, to the team, if one or two people have let the side down. You can always coach them separately and always remember to try to remain positive. As a manager, with your coaching hat on, you should always be aware that it may be something you have done incorrectly or forgotten that has caused the issues.

You should also always have firmly in your minds that a team is full of egos'. Each member of your team may believe that they are the next Manager and may want all the high profile jobs and projects, the best training and the most focus on development. Try to share out the high profile stuff, give each team member an equal chance and never compare one member with another. By all means use examples of how something has been done, but don't make out that another person's way is better than theirs. It is simply an alternative they may want to consider.

In my ASA teaching course, I had to coach some children in a group, in parallel with others on the course doing the same. I took my group and separated them by ability and coached the split down groups accordingly. As a result, the slower or less experienced ones didn't hold back the development of the others. One of the other coaches, adjacent to where I was working hadn't done that and his group were all working at the rate of the slowest and less competent swimmer. The course tutor berated him for it and pointed at what I was doing, making a direct comparison. This was not great teaching. The comparison factor would weigh heavily upon the guy being berated. *'I'm not as good as him.'* He would instantly believe he was second rate because of that comparison. It put me in an awkward position as a potential 'teacher's pet' and destroyed the guy's confidence, to do anything else without verification. A better move would have been to ask why he thought the class were not developing as quickly as he might have hoped and then asked him to have a look at some of the other groups to see if he could spot anything he could do to improve the situation.

There is also one other essential element to consider, in relation to individuals, when coaching a team. The place they occupy. In football, if you have a player who scores a lot of goals, don't believe that his success is purely down to his ability, talent and genius. Look at how he gets those goals. Is it the service he is getting from the rest of the team? Are they playing to his strengths? Are others creating the space he needs to take full advantage? Is it the coach – i.e. you - who has done something to motivate and develop that talent in the player?

In business, it could be just the same. A successful manager may rely on a couple of good team members or an administrator, giving him the information he needs to do his job well. He may have a really strong team of self-starters who are ambitious and diligent. Contrast that with a manager who has to spend a lot of time coaching and counselling his staff. Who is going to smell more strongly of roses? Who is doing the best job?

You have to be aware of the player and the team relationship. In my school team, I started off as a defender, basically because I didn't think I'd get a run up front. I lacked confidence and had been told that there were some good guys; better than me, up front already. I played in defence for half the season, timing my interventions and tackles brilliantly, and knocking the ball well clear up field, most of the time to one of our team. It was quite a good period, and I enjoyed being a good solid defender. However, I may have mentioned a couple of times that I normally played up front and eventually, the teacher in charge decided to give me a go. In the first five minutes of the game, some thirty five to forty yards out, I cracked a shot towards the goal. I say shot; it was more like one of my defensive clearances. It flew into the goal, leaving the bewildered keeper stranded on the edge of the six yard box. Having moved up front and displaced one of the 'regulars' I wasn't particularly well liked. As such, I didn't get the ball passed to me that often. My success, relative to how I had been perceived in defence, was poor. I moved back into defence a few games later, deemed a failure by those who originally berated me. The following year I began playing for my father's works team and played up front. I came on as a substitute in the first game and scored within fifteen minutes of my arrival. My father was well liked and respected; I had just scored an equalising goal. I played for them in that position for three years and saw plenty of the ball.

In business, you will get the same cultural difficulties. If the person is not introduced into the team properly, does not fit in, is seen to replace someone popular or is not a likeable person, they will not be engaged properly, will not be communicated with fully. People will avoid or delay dealing with them and that will have an impact on the job. As a coach, you have two elements to tackle; the person and the team. You will need to ask yourself the question, "Have I made the right choice?" Have you erred in the cultural and professional fit? There may be a variety of other reasons why that person is not engaged or the team seem to avoid them. You will have to tease out the reasons and deal with them. The problem is not necessarily that of the individual, it could simply be the culture your team dynamic has created, in which case you need to alter the dynamic, not the culture.

4.6. Individual Coaching

There are positives and negatives to coaching an individual, as opposed to a team. The obvious positives are that you can develop a closer relationship and focus more attention on the individual, but the downside will be that there will be a greater expectation on results and achievement. Coaching a team, you rely on all members pulling their weight and responding to the coaching, with an individual, you only have one to worry about.

In sport, the coach can be a defining factor in relation to the success of the individual. This is also true for individuals in business. If you consider the sports where a one-on-one, coach to player, relationship matters the most, these are usually intense sports where the player or participant is out on their own once the event starts. Tennis is a prime example. The player can often be out there, expected to perform, for several hours, with few breaks and virtually no contact from the coach. I say virtually as, no doubt, body language and facial expressions will speak volumes. It can be a very lonely place if things are not going your way.

In business, you will come across situations which are similar, but a member of your team or someone you are coaching can always pick up a phone, or drop you an email, if they need guidance. It is more a question of how confident they are in their own judgement and, to an extent, how effective your previous coaching has been.

Although not a coach, a golfer's caddy can advise and discuss the tactics of the match with the player. I often used to think it strange that the top exponents of this game had people to carry their clubs, who were evidently not as talented, but who would also advise them on the shot and which club to use. Is it positive affirmation? Is it a lack of confidence in the choice? What if the caddy is wrong? In business the Caddy could be a sort of coaching figure or mentor, perhaps a peer whom a colleague can turn to, to read through an email or run an idea by. It is not necessarily advice you will use, but it is almost always welcome and another point of view. As a manager, just asking the 'caddie' to read through a missive you have written or check over a presentation can be a form of effective coaching. They will feel valued, they will feel that their opinion is worth something and be more involved at the level you are working. Often, it is that sort of engagement which leads to a team member being coached to take that extra step-up.

The best thing about individual coaching is that you can obtain faster and more impressive results if the target of the coaching is receptive, positive and trusts you entirely. Some coaches have a skill in the actual coaching which is greater than their ability to actually do the things they coach in. Where they excel is in their ability to listen, watch and interpret what the sportsperson or business colleague is doing and then to translate that into coaching points. It is paramount to establish a relationship with the individual being coached which will allow those particular strengths to be used unfettered.

This is also another area where there is a significant difference between teaching and coaching. I would ask you to consider first, the old George Bernard Shaw quote, which I have always found a little insulting to those who don the gown and mortar board, the quote goes, "Those who can, do, those who can't, teach." It implies that those who teach cannot actually apply their acquired knowledge into a practical environment, such as a business role. It is really quite a smear, when you consider that the definition of intelligence is the application of acquired knowledge.

In Shaw's day, possibly all teachers went from school, to University or College, then back to School to teach and therefore never really saw anything of the 'real' world. In my experience, the best Teachers we had at School were those who had started in industry of some sort then moved into teaching later. In coaching though, things are different. Yes, you can be a good coach, if you have never competed in a sport. Yes you can develop someone in business, to go beyond and exceed your own achievements. Coaching is not, as I have said previously, about putting something in; it is about bringing something out. This doesn't mean either that it is simply a case of bringing something out, which has previously been taught. Some individuals have what is referred to as, a natural talent. They may not realise it. It may manifest itself in a manner unconnected to how the coach may ultimately use it. There are quite a few high profile examples of this in sport, where a youngster is spotted competing in one sport, and slightly better than average, but because there are transferrable natural abilities involved, a coach from another sport re-directs them with phenomenal results. It is about recognising and seeing the potential, but then being able to work with that individual to fully exploit it.

Anthony Alozie was a soccer player in a local team in Nigeria. He became involved in running when an athletics coach saw his turn of pace at a soccer game. Alozie and the coach corresponded and eventually he was convinced he had a talent in sprinting. In the 2009 world championships, Alozie placed third in the 4x100m relay with team mates Matt Davies, Josh Ross and Aaron Rouge-Serret, their seasons' best time of 38.93 not enough to advance to the final. At the 2011 world championships he raced the 4x100m and clocked 38.69 for fourth in the heat. Perhaps not world beating success, but certainly placing him high in the top echelons of sprinting, rather than just being yet another quick soccer player.

In business, we can quite often overlook someone's natural ability, because they are in a role that doesn't necessarily bring it out. This is where a lot of your skill as a coach can be at its most effective. I would advocate looking at the colleague's CV more closely. One technique I employ when recruiting and trawling through CV's is not to look at the business experience first, but cut straight to the hobbies and personal interests section. You may ask why? CV's are generally embellished as we have already observed. For example, a line like, 'Responsible for safe and efficient storage and retrieval of sensitive data files,' could be interpreted with one simple word; filing. People will do this to dress up some of the more mundane tasks they perform, but look at what they do outside work and it is likely that they are good at it; proud of it; have a talent for it and probably enjoy it. So why not look at that as an indicator of what they are actually like? I once saw a rather boring CV from a guy who had applied to work in our team. The work experience and education bit was just like thousands of others. His hobbies and interests section though was inspirational. He played five different instruments, two of them semi-professionally. He had completed almost all the Munroe's (Scottish Mountains over 3000 ft, of which there are 282) and had taken part in an endurance Marathon in the Sahara. So what did that tell me? He was determined, he liked and could rise to a challenge; he could assimilate detailed and complex instructions into practical use. He was dogged and would stick at a task. He could follow a rigid programme of development and learning to a high level. Add all that up and you have yourself a great hands-on Project Coordinator, to start with. Coaching and development could get him to Programme Manager level without too much sweat. He had applied to be a Service Desk Operator. As far as I know he is now a contract Project Manager, working on a varied portfolio of I.T. Projects. His hobbies and interests changed his life, by giving us a glimpse of his potential.

I suppose that little example is an indicator that we should know our people pretty well, as coaches, particularly if we are coaching on a one-to-one basis.

One other quite important area to be aware of, as a sports coach, is the world stage and what is happening in other countries. There may be new techniques or approaches which you can adopt or adapt, but more importantly, you will be able to define your targets. It is pointless training and coaching a swimmer to achieve a personal best of 48 seconds for 100 metres freestyle, if in Australia they have people swimming consistently three seconds faster. You have to set the bar higher and try to match the best.

In business, the same has to apply, although it may be about a number of elements rather than simply performance. It might be, for example, about operating costs, it might be about adopting new technology. The global market is now much more important to be aware of and constantly assess than it ever was. Developing individuals to learn new techniques and processes and how to better manage the key components of what they are responsible for has to be on a global scale. The competition is no longer local; it is the World.

4.7. Give a fish, teach to fish...

'Give a man a fish, and you feed him for a day; show him how to catch fish, and you feed him for a lifetime.'

It is a proverb you may have heard and quite a sound observation. Most business people would like to be independent and not have to be effectively spoon fed when doing their jobs. There is, on the other side of the coin, also the need to shy away from being too preachy or even too 'teachy'. I knew someone who spent two hours teaching a new recruit the best way to answer the telephone. The new recruit lasted three days. The lesson is to reach and coach a level of independence, which you feel they will be comfortable with.

This applies, when in the context of business or sport, you are looking to teach someone how to coach, or even self coach.

Consider the golfer again. He goes out on a practice round, without his coach to hand and tries to put into practice all the things he has been coached on, to date. If he makes a mistake, how does he know? It might be a 'results based' or outcomes based judgement. For example, he's hit the ball straight and long and put it into a great approach spot on the fairway. He feels good about it, but he just has a little nagging doubt that he missed something. The round proceeds and he's hitting great shots, consistently, but he still has that nagging doubt.

The problem is that, if he continues to play well, but is doing something wrong, it could become a habit. He might have been fortunate that on this particular day, it has gone well, but another day, he might not be so lucky. What should he do?

Actually, it is not down to him to make that decision. His coach should have made that one for him, before he went out on the course. The ideal scenario would have been that the coach would assess him, before he went out on his own. He would then give the golfer a couple of coaching points; things to work on, and nothing else. In the sixth form at School, we young gentlemen were allowed to select Golf as an option in the summer for our Games lesson. We were professionally coached by the Club Assistant Pro Golfer. The one thing I can remember about him, aside from his arrogance, was that he always started us off on a round of Golf with a couple of coaching points. One week, for example, he took all the clubs out of our bags except a seven iron and a putter, and made us do the whole round with just those. The coaching points were to learn how to use the available tools and get used to being able to hit by degrees. In other words, don't always go full strength with your shots, gauge how much power you need to hit with, not what you can hit with. As far as I can remember, my scorecard for that round was just as good as when I had a full bag to choose from; amazing.

It is the same in most sports, as it is in business, when the individual is away, off the blocks, they are on their own. What they take with them into a meeting, a project or a race; is down to the coaching you have given them. You have in effect, taught them to fish.

It should be self evident why this is important. In coaching, you are looking to improve performance, but you are also aiming to promote self help and independence. There is no more-lonely a place for a Tennis player, than out on that court, a set and two breaks down, but you see it time and time again in the top players. From what appears to be an irretrievable position, they come back, often winning the match. It is not just about their brilliance, stamina and determination. It is the strength and value of their coaching that has finally kicked in. Something has triggered as they focus in those rest periods, as they run through rallies and positional plays in their head, something has come back to them; try that.

In business, we want our teams and our reports to think on their feet and not come asking for advice all the time. There is nothing wrong with them if they do. It is again, probably our fault.

In some situations, they will find themselves with just a seven iron and a putter in their bag. What are they going to do; whine? Or learn to hit with what they have? You have to prepare them for those situations. Talk through the job, just like the Golf coach might talk through the round, one shot at a time. Let them come up with the answers too, it will show that they are thinking about the potential problems and even if they are wrong sometimes, at least that is a positive sign.

Earlier I mentioned a big project I was involved in, a few years back, where I had to fly down to a meeting in London each week. A lot of the work on this project was undertaken, on the ground, over the weekends. When the project started, for the first five or six weeks, my Saturdays and Sundays were spent glued to my Nokia 6570. A seemingly, endless stream of questions were flying in from all directions and I had to make a decision on every single one of them. Had that continued for the duration of the project, I would have been burned out at about month fifteen. I had to get smarter and deal with it. I looked at the type of queries I was being bombarded with and the solutions I had come up with. There was a pattern. It was quite a simple one. As there were several similar jobs ongoing at any one time, perhaps twenty, and the same end result was desirable in each one, I coached the team leaders out on these jobs in what it was we were aiming to do; the one single, ultimate outcome that we wanted in each job. I then instructed them like this. *'As long as you achieve that desired outcome, even if it means we revisit later and have a process of refinement, if you get an issue, you take whatever action you see fit and let me know what you've done in an e-mail.'* The desired outcome is not important, neither are the specifics of what the project was. The fact was I had prepared them to go off the blocks and swim for themselves. They were on the Golf course with only two clubs to play with. The number of calls at the weekend reduced dramatically, my emails grew a little, but the net result was that jobs were completed seamlessly to any observer. No one knew that they had been a set and two breaks down; they just became pragmatists, dealt with it and moved on. In my

Tuesday meetings I was then able to relax a little, with data at my fingertips. I could give updates along the lines of, *'We had an issue with data cabling at this location, but the engineer was able to draw a temporary cable in to place to get things working. We will revisit later to attend to the faulty cabling.'* I looked and sounded like I was in control, there had been no mad panic on site, with frantic telephone calls over the weekend. I had my life back.

We talk about empowering people. Most people would believe that this is about giving responsibility and accountability. It isn't always the case. Sometimes it is about giving people the coaching and the confidence to do what they feel is right. This becomes much easier if they understand and accept what it is you are trying to achieve. If we go back to the Golf coach again, when he set us off with just those two clubs, he didn't say that he expected us to match our scorecards to when we had a full bag of clubs. He just wanted us to learn to feel that we could vary the power and get more out of the clubs we had. My suspicion was that, had he not been so prescriptive, we would have tried to match our cards and ended up having an appalling round. Think of empowerment as liberation, not as accountability. Think of it as a seven iron and a putter. Use what you have to the best possible effect.

All of which brings us back neatly to the title of this section. If you are going to teach someone to fish, metaphorically speaking, remember that there are several ways in which to fish, not just one. You might go for the rod and line, but what about a net on a long pole, or one that you cast, like a Shabakeh? What about a trawl net or a fixed net, which you empty later? Make it clear to them that there are many ways in which to take away coaching points and use them depending upon the circumstances and situations they might find themselves in. Don't just stick to one tried and trusted process.

4.8. Technique and speed

Earlier we talked about briefly about Wing Chung and how the technique is practiced very slowly and controlled to begin with, then gradually speeded up as strength and movement is effectively programmed in to the muscles. A similar approach is adopted in Swimming, Golf and a few other sports. Getting those basic shapes and movements accurate, shifting the weight and making them natural and smooth, rather than considered and jerky, is a key part of making them work effectively.

At this stage, coaching is all about correcting the movements and the stance and weight distribution. It is about balance and co-ordination. If these are not right or are neglected before you move on, there will be weak elements in the performance, some of which will be harder to correct later. In effect, what we are doing is establishing norms. In swimming, you will coach a breaststroker to reach forward as they kick and affect a glide, before they hit catch and then begin their pull. It is the kick and glide which makes the stroke efficient. A novice can go from thirty Strokes for a 25 metre swim down to under ten, simply by correcting that particular element. They might be slower, but energy wise, they have used far less.

If we establish this as the only way to do that stroke then begin to speed it up, that is where we will begin to see the ultimate goal being achieved. The execution becomes faster, the glide element less obvious, but it is still there and with it comes a much more fluid and effective fast stroke. It is that focus on the technique and the insistence that this has to be ground in, if ultimately we want a fast and competitive swim.

Only by setting and establishing those norms will you find later that the higher levels of achievement are attained. You need to be patient and allow the speed to be acquired over a period of time. I have seen young swimmers, aged between 7 and 10, learn and adopt beautiful, flowing and effective technique, only to ditch it in favour of a fast and inefficient stroke in a competitive swim. They are caught up in the moment and watch others go off twenty to the dozen and they follow, believing they will be left far behind. In reality, those who go off like that will tire and the ones who use what they have learned and practiced will still have plenty of energy left for the last 10 metres.

Consider again the golfer. Nice smooth swing, good stance and body weight transfer. On the tee though, the devil takes over and he wants to knock the cover off it. Result; he tops it and it trickles for thirty yards. You have to keep coaching people on that control, on the basics and on the establishment of their technique as the foundation on which everything is built.

In business, it is just as important. Disciplines and techniques are there to be adopted and used. Only by ensuring that they are will you prevent the potential disasters lurking silently for an opportunity to raise their ugly heads.

Many years ago, we concluded that the most vulnerable time for our systems and infrastructure was during change. I'm sure that is no surprise to you. We did not operate any sort of formal change control and if there was a problem, we were largely at the mercy of someone remembering that someone else had made a change or being sharp enough to spot that one had been made.

In an attempt to reign in this behaviour, we cobbled together a change request process and a mechanism for approval. There was quite a bit of resistance, mainly from the application teams. Their argument was that, it could take five minutes to complete the change process, take a further 30-60 minutes to gain approval and all to complete a change that would actually take thirty seconds to implement. The counter argument was that, yes it might take five minutes to complete now, but once they had completed a few, that time would reduce significantly. Familiarity with the process would also reduce the approval time and ultimately, what it would mean, would be that, if a change did cause an issue, we could quickly identify it and back it out. Nothing was more graphically illustrated than an incident which occurred around that time. A member of the application team made a change that disturbed a sub-routine in a key programme. The programme ran overnight and at 02:00 hrs it stopped processing. Fortunately the OPC Scheduler alerted someone to the failure and the Application team programmer was called out. He dialled in and it took him an hour to find and rectify the issue. From start to finish the delay was two hours twenty minutes and then the programme resumed and finished, but missing the following mornings' deadlines. As a result, supplier orders were late going out and vital sales data not available. The application programmer who made the change had not completed the change process and that is why it took so long to spot the error; a missing semi-colon in a line of code. We estimated the cost of that particular debacle at around £20,000.

It is also worth considering how established and well practiced methods of doing things give people re-assurances. If it has worked many times before, there is a fair chance it will work again. We created a template for opening a retail outlet. It was a programme of works covering a number of weeks from survey to opening and it was detailed and comprehensive. The first few times we implemented it, it seemed to be a labour. After that it became an absolute necessity. It also meant that, virtually anyone could pick it up and run with it. As an unexpected bonus we found that, if we needed to accelerate it, we could with very little tweaking, because nothing was missing and dependencies were clearly identified.

In sport also, the control and impact of change, no matter how small, must be assessed and considered. Football managers do this during a game. They are on the losing side, ten minutes into the second half and their strategy is not working. They want to make a couple of personnel changes to try a different approach. They have to consider how those changes will affect the whole dynamic of the team. It can be a huge gamble, but many times, particularly with the more successful managers and coaches, their changes seem inspired and pay off. Interestingly, it is the most experienced managers who seem to get these 'snap' decisions to work for them. Why do we think that might be? In my view it is because they are not snap decisions. They are just good, fast decisions, made with brilliant technique. They see where it is going wrong. They assess what they need to do to fix it, they brief the players being introduced and they somehow communicate to the remainder of the team how to re-organise themselves so that the changes will work effectively. This is not something you can do without learning over a period of time how these changes might work and, yes, getting it wrong sometimes.

In business, as in sport, most of the time, timing is everything. If you have good technique and can execute what you want to do quickly, you can take advantage of the moment; seize the opportunity. If you are still learning the ropes and making sure your moves are accurate, rather than expedient, don't worry, but be aware of the opportunities you will be able to take later.

Going back to the Wing Chung, my son was attacked in his workplace, by two drug fuelled individuals. His great technique and speed dispatched both of them to the ground and effectively subdued them in, just under, two seconds; I know because I saw the CCTV footage. Those students of his who diligently work through those movements painstakingly and slowly, should take some comfort that at some future point, their speed, accuracy and effectiveness will all come together like that.

4.9. That lethal combination

Every now and then there is a happy union of great coach and great individual or team. This is as true in sport as it is in business, but perhaps in the latter it is not recognised as such. Talented sports coaches and sports-people coming together to form that lethal combination is highly visible and much applauded. Great business combinations, when they occur, are maybe not so visible and not particularly celebrated in the same way. The top companies' boardrooms are bristling with dynamism and talent, when they are inspired and lead by someone equally as dynamic and talented is when you get that extra buzz.

We can probably all quote examples of great coach/team/star relationships in sport. My own personal memories from growing up are from the great Leeds United team of the 60's and 70's and their manager Don Revie. Whilst many people criticised the way that team played and some of Revie's tactics, there was still little doubt that it was a great combination and many of the players of that era are still revered as some of the greatest to play the beautiful game. In the modern day, you cannot deny the remarkable longevity of football managers like Arsene Wenger at Arsenal and of course Sir Alex Ferguson at Manchester United. Whilst many managers at that level are lucky to survive a few seasons at a club, these guys are on track for a long service clock! So what is it about them that make them as coaches, and the teams they build, which sets them apart?

Whilst being very different in their personalities and outlook, they are both superb readers of the game, recognisers of talent and both have an uncanny ability to find players who can fit seamlessly into the dynamic they create.

In business, we see the 'movers and shakers' trading places all the time. In fact, it seems that, if you stay in one place for too long, you are looked upon as a bit of a failure. It hasn't always been that way and really, it isn't always down to a desire to move onwards and upwards. It is usually about results. If you don't hit the targets set for you, the door will be left ajar for your exit. So why should that be so? What is wrong with putting a team together that can stay the course; that can have some continuity and can regenerate itself piece by piece as time progresses? The answer is nothing. It just doesn't seem to happen anymore in large organisations.

The real coaching starts once the initial 80% of the work is out of the way. Once you have your talented individual or team in that final 20% improvements become increasingly harder to achieve and the goal setting and targeting of achievement through coaching starts to reach the macro level. Consider the swimmer, heading to be in the upper echelons of the 100 metre freestyle swimmers in the world. The World's best will be breaking the fifty second barrier frequently, in pursuit of a World record some five seconds or so faster than that. Our swimmer, through top coaching and training gets to the fifty five second mark over a period of time and is now in that last 20%. The goal setting and targeting of what they do and how they do it becomes more detailed, more intense and the steps smaller and more frequent. The coaching will focus on tiny observations, scientific adjustments and the application of technique to almost perfection as seconds then hundreds of a second are chipped away. Similarly, in our Golfing example, bringing down that handicap, first to scratch and then beyond into the negatives will be all about detail. Better shot selection, better touch and feel, reading the course and conditions, maintaining the concentration right through the stroke. Minute changes in posture, speed, weight transfer could put the ball ten metres past or to the left or right of where you wanted it to end up, and that could mean a shot dropped. If you think about a golfer hitting a shot with professional accuracy, in the same terms as a marksman with a rifle, a tiny shift at the source, where the ball or the bullet is discharged and it can be a country mile adrift at the target end. It all has to be very scientific and precise.

So, what do we do in business, generally? We set a goal like "Reduce your operating cost by 5% this year." We may revisit that cost along the way, to see if we are getting near to the mark, but we don't coach on it, we don't break it down and we certainly don't view it as a failing on our part if our team member fails to deliver it. That goal, by sporting standards is a blunt instrument. It's the sporting equivalent of saying to a Soccer team, 'I want you to score seven today guys,' then beating them up at the end of the match because they only scored five. We have to look at these things more objectively and break them down, and then make them into achievable steps. Instead of throwing that arbitrary 5% statement into the objectives, why not look at the whole picture and suggest areas where savings could be made – *"I think if you look at the support at these sites, we might be paying over the odds. Some of the kit is old. Why not look at a refresh programme and see if that reduces the support costs?"* Isn't that better than the earlier goal? It gives them something to look at and target, which may give them other ideas to follow up and it's measurable and quantifiable.

I was given an objective one year to develop one of my team to allow his promotion to the next level. That was it, just that. Had I been clueless, that objective would have floored me completely. Fortunately, I was able to break it down, look at the guy's strengths, identify his weaknesses and work out a plan to improve the former and really strengthen the latter. He didn't even know it was happening. It was gradual, staged into neat small steps and with achievable and measurable targets. When we reached the point where he was suggesting what we should do next, I knew we were almost there. It is a really good feeling.

I suppose the message is, to think more like a sportsman would when looking at objectives and goals. When you break that record, that may have been the goal you set out to achieve, but now it's in the past, now you can set a new goal, to be faster, jump further, higher or whatever. It doesn't stop just because you hit that target. All the top business achievers share those characteristics with top sports people. The current goal is just a target to hit; it is not the end of the road. There will be a new goal immediately that one is achieved.

I am also a firm believer that there are two distinct types of achiever in sport, and that must also be true in business. The really top, record breaking performers, even those who become legends, do not make the best coaches. They may have the greatest talent, to do what they do, but they cannot translate that into coaching. The best coaches seem to be those whom have tasted high level success, but were not necessarily exalted for it. Think of the great football players, the big names, they tend to go into higher administrative management of clubs or their own businesses, rather than back to the coal face as coaches. The truly great coaches come from the solid dependable defenders and the industrious midfielders. They tend to be those who were, just there, in great teams and perhaps to a degree, unsung. Think about Golf. The Club Professionals coach all the time, the playing professionals aim to win big money tournaments, they don't become coaches. We have to ask why that should be. After all, as a great player, you could still continue to earn big money as a great coach, long after your playing days have finished. So why are there not more high profile names in sports coaching after they hang up their boots?

We have looked at what makes a great coach. What makes a great performer? The answer is somewhere in the T.A.S.K. analysis as we said earlier, although the difference in the two is in the 'Person' section.

A great athlete or sports star may have the dedication to be brilliant at what they do, but not to be a great leader or coach. They may have come from a background or culture which has nurtured a need or desire to help people. They may be motivated and enthusiastic to share what they have acquired and learned. Look at the person and not necessarily their talent or skill as a player or business manager. They have always been and will always be that person, whatever it is they are doing.

In chapter four we have looked at some of the artistic elements we can use when coaching, but to effect delivery in a scientific way. Our approach should not be stilted and appear scripted, but natural and flowing. We should be fully aware of how not to de-motivate, in our body language or expressions, we should develop a relationship that allows us to be honest, without being negative and we should encourage those being coached to be self critical. We have looked at what makes a good coach and there is enough to be going on with to get to that point. We have also looked at what makes a great coach, something we should all aspire to.

We have looked at the difference between coaching teams and individuals, taking care not to be general in our comments and coaching points, but without excluding anyone. We have also discussed the ultimate in self help, developing the mind set which makes the coachees start to examine their own performance and not be afraid of some autonomy in what they do. We have also examined improving technique and speed and when those two should be addressed as part of a coaching programme. Finally, we looked at that lethal combination of great team or individual and great coach. This is a truly unstoppable force, when it comes together and should be aspired to by all who coach.

CHAPTER 5.
THE ART IN THE SCIENCE OF COACHING

This time we are looking at the science of coaching and where the art comes in. So, we have to ask the question, what is art? People have many definitions of it but essentially, in any form it is about representation, interpretation and proportion. A great coach will be a scientist, but also an artist. A great coach will take the science in coaching and in the subject matter, whether that is sport or business, and use representation, interpret the principles in an innovative way and yet still keep the proportions right. Above all a great coach will work in a very tight, ordered and structured way, adhering to principles and well practiced and refined techniques, but still make it look like he's winging it. There is a story that Leonardo Da Vinci gained entry to Art school by drawing a perfect circle freehand. This is a great example of what I am talking about if it is indeed true. Only a scholar who fully understands the science of geometry could be such an accomplished and skilled artist.

There are many examples of that kind of crossover in this chapter, where the edges are slightly blurred between the two, until you realise that they are one and the same thing, but perhaps opposite ends. To be a great coach, you have to know much about coaching techniques and practice them all the time, but equally you have to know people, your people. If coaching is a Science, the art is in its execution.

Creativity is something which people talk about in terms of art. What about being creative in your coaching? It will make it memorable. If creativity becomes a norm, something practiced and executed so often that it is automatic, then there will be a difference in the whole game. You can still be scientific in your creativity; you have to be, otherwise it will not work.

In the following sections we will explore a few areas usually discussed in sport, but which are foundations of the way we should coach people to think about their work, to be creative.

5.1. First touch

I moved from one Primary School to another when I was nine years old. Most kids who played football with any conviction, made it in the School football team when they were ten years old. At my previous School, my place had been assured, being one of the better players and one who really wanted to play. When I moved schools, things did not appear to be that clear cut. The master who looked after the team had a clear idea of who was likely to make the team before I arrived and nothing was going to change that. He did, though, give me a trial, to see if I was good enough.

This consisted of him calling me over, during a 'games session', producing one of the old brown footballs with laces in it, and tapping it to me, with a brief instruction that I should tap it back to him. This I did with a variable measure of accuracy, as the ball bobbled on the rough ground and the laces did their best to exaggerate that. I wasn't told that this was my trial. I had never undergone any such exercise before and yet, based on his judgement of my ability in this 'skill', I didn't make the team.

In the months that followed, as we 'no-hopers' were pitted against the so called elite in our 'games' lessons, my ability shone through. I scored against them frequently. I could tackle most of them, quite easily and outrun half of them. So why did the 'coach' not select me for the team?

To me, it was clear that I had as much actual game play talent as anyone in the team. I couldn't therefore understand why I had not been selected, even after my regular weekly displays. At length, I asked the team captain, what it was all about. Was it because I was the new boy? Was it because he had, effectively already picked his team? The answer I received was a little bit of a surprise. The captain indicated that the little test, I had been put through, was to assess my first touch.

Apparently, you can tell a lot about a footballer, rugby player, hockey player, by their first touch. It is that combination of being able to receive, control and play, all in one slick movement that defines the players overall ability. I still maintain that, once a game was in progress, you would have been hard pressed to pick me out as a player with a poor first touch, but evidently, those were the coach's criteria.

For eighteen months I worked on my first touch. I kicked the ball high in the air, against walls everything I could think of then went to control it, bring it down and make a play. As a result, when I moved Schools, I did get into the team, but the evidence to support the first touch principle didn't fully hit me until a few years later. I started to play for my father's workplace team when I was fifteen. We were a reasonable outfit, but not great. One week we played a team from the Leeds Police and they had a player who had allegedly had trials with a few top clubs. It was clear that he was in a different league to the rest of us. One thing made it abundantly clear. Yes; it was his first touch. Long high balls played to him at pace were just plucked out of the air. All the sting of pace and direction removed and the next move expertly executed, whether it was wrong footing one of us, or playing a killer first time pass, he had it all. I can still picture one particular move now. I was in awe.

Move on fifteen years or so and I'm watching a match between Gomersal and Farsley; two local teams to where I live. The difference is that these are the under elevens and in one of the teams, is my work-mates son, Lee.

Lee was brought on with a quarter of an hour left, with the scores tied at 1-1. He demonstrated perfectly what the Primary school coach had been looking for. His first goal of three, in those fifteen minutes, was just pure class. The winger hit a diagonal ball across the box, right to left. Lee was at the left corner of the box, some 25 yards from goal. In one deft movement he trapped it, tapped it a few inches to his right and struck it with the outside of his foot into the top corner. Once again, that was the difference. The two other goals he scored were testament to the power of that first touch, the control, the vision and the execution.

Now, after all this prattle about football and why my football career never quite moved from lower league on Saturday afternoons, I expect you are wondering where the 'first touch' in business comes in?

It is an often used phrase, first impressions are lasting ones. It is true. Psychologists will tell you that we make our minds up about people in thirty seconds. Whether that is true or not, your approach to a piece of work, your opening address in a meeting or even the way you say good morning, all exhibit those first touch principles. In a few seconds you can impart confidence, enthusiasm and get people's attention, or you can effectively give the ball away. If you don't inspire, exude positivity and control you will have lost the game before you really begin.

So how do we coach that for our teams and how do we practice it ourselves? What do we need to do to ensure that our people have a great first touch and can read the game well? What do we need to do ourselves to demonstrate that all the time?

No matter what you think about your performance during a piece of work, you should think about your 'first touch'. Equally, you should coach your teams and your reports to think about it too. It would be easy to be glib about it and just say what we've said already and let you work it out. However, I don't believe in being glib, so let's look at what we mean by first touch in sport and break it down, so that we can compare those elements against what we might encounter in the business world.

In Golf, it might be about looking at the hole you are about to play and your club choice. It might go as far as the way you position the ball on the tee and address it. In Swimming, it might be the way you engage with the blocks as you push off for that racing dive and even as far as the underwater kick and glide to get you started. In football, as we have said already, it is about taking that pass, controlling it and being ready to do the next thing, whether that is another pass, a shot or a great piece of dribbling. In essence preparation, control, execution. These are things we have covered before, but as elements we should adopt within a piece of work, or in our working day. In this example they are specific to the commencement of a piece of work. The equivalent of a great drive, hitting a great point on the fairway, where you can chip to the green. It might be a powerful and shallow dive, getting you up there with the leaders for when the full stroke starts. Or it could be a killer pass, first time, to a team member in space.

Coach Preparation, Planning, Anticipate questions, Have a structure to the work, be able to articulate clearly how you expect it to play out.

Coach Control, You are the one calling the shots. You have a good grasp of what is going to happen, when how and by whom.

Coach Execution, Professionalism, Clarity, Accuracy, Focus.

The difference between a lower league performer and a Premier League performer is about their ability to take ownership of a piece of work right from the start and leave everyone else in no doubt about who is in the driving seat. They should inspire confidence, be able to disseminate and assign tasks and define clear and achievable goals. In other words, be realistic.

I have, as usual, a perfect example of the opposite. I was briefly involved in the start of a project a few years back, which was replacing the end to end of a legacy system. I won't say much more than that the front end and the back end were both being changed out, as were elements like payment methods and accounting system interfaces. In the kick off meeting, where all the people involved in elements of the work were invited along, the Project Manager and Technical Architects gave a top line view of what was being done, why and how, with a rough idea on timescales. I asked, what I thought was an obvious question, at the end of the presentation, as it had not been covered. I asked if we could see the end to end design, side by side with the current design, so we could see where elements were changing and what was affected. They didn't have one. Not only that, despite people saying that they felt that sort of view would be an asset, they didn't have one in subsequent meetings.

I began to have serious reservations about their ability to deliver, as did others. Work started to be done in silos by different development teams and infrastructure teams. The Project Managers and Technical Architects still didn't pull everything together. Their first touch let the ball run loose. I liken it to the old cartoon of the guys building the Railroad across the USA. One group starts on the east side, the other on the west and eventually they meet up in the middle to find that the tracks don't quite come together. You could see quite clearly, as an observer, what was going to happen and it had all begun with that first touch. Ultimately, someone had to take over the Project and set the stall out properly. By this time, a good year had been wasted in misconceptions, poor design and invalid assumptions. The two years that the project was supposed to take, went out of the window and it eventually took almost four years. I reckon if they had spent a couple of weeks before the kick-off canvassing views on what people expected to see in the actual initiation meeting they would have saved a good portion of those additional two years.

It is not just about large projects though. The day to day approach to any work can be affected by that first touch, the initial reaction to a problem or incident; people looking for a solution before they know and understand the extent of the issue. It wastes time, it is wasted effort and it doesn't get you any nearer. The first thing to do here is to listen. You shouldn't need to coach people in listening, but you will have to at some point. There is a natural tendency for people to want to be heard in meetings and this may manifest itself with a kind of premature ejaculation; speculative, not fully fact based and a quite feeble attempt to be heard. Coach your guys and yourself to listen more. Make notes, look for clues. Ask questions, but listen to the answers. Ultimately, you will find yourself in a better place than if you had just rifled off a few ill-conceived thoughts.

There is, of course, one absolutely unarguable result from having and demonstrating a great first touch. To use the football analogy again, you will have more balls played your way. People will knock the ball to you, knowing that you will be able to control it and do something with it. You become, in business terms, a safe pair of hands.

5.2. Look for space

"Ability is nothing without opportunity." Napoleon.

In the sixth form at School, we had a Deputy Head Master who was really into his Football. He became the coach of the school team and developed an awesome unit, which made its way to the FA Schools Trophy Yorkshire Finals, only to be robbed of national exposure in a replayed game after a draw. What was exceptional about his coaching amounted to two things. Firstly, he encouraged people to play their own game, but as part of the team. He moved people into positions where they became more comfortable, but perhaps hadn't considered playing before.

Example; There was a guy with a mean right foot who played on the right. This meant that when he was coming in on goal, any shot he might take was generally going to go wide to the left or rise into row 25, because he was not striking across it enough. The solution was to move him to the left and encourage him, when in possession, to cut inside and have a shot at goal. By doing that simple thing, the player often found himself with space, at an angle to the goal, where he could strike across the ball better and hit the target.

Similarly, he gave the team two extremely simple rules to follow. If we're in possession and you don't have the ball, within your shape, look for a space and run into it. If you do have the ball, knock it into space. More often than not, once we had assimilated those coaching tips, we found that we were receiving the ball in space and could move the ball about with much more confidence. In time, it became instinctive. You would know, from the way a player played and the position they occupied in the shape, where they were likely to be in two or three seconds' time. In other words, the space you were aiming the ball at. It was a kind of magic that left opposing teams spellbound.

Years later, I found myself in a situation where my daughters Under 11, seven a side team, were due to play in a competition, but the Coach hadn't turned up (he had to work at short notice), and two of their players hadn't arrived either. Knowing I was a Swimming Coach at the time, a few of the other parents nominated me to take over the team for the day, which I was reluctant to do, but I eventually succumbed to the five pleading faces, looking up at me. When we arrived at the competition, we checked that we would still be allowed to play with just five players. That was acceptable, so we then prepared to do battle. The first team we were to play offered us two players, to make it even. I asked the girls what they wanted to do. They unanimously decided they would play as a five, which immediately made me feel better. If they felt like that, they didn't feel at a disadvantage and wanted to play, we were 80% there.

I had never watched them play previously with any thoughts of how they played. I had just stood and bellowed until I was hoarse. So I decided that, after a few random words of encouragement, I'd assess the first half and see if there was anything I could do to avert a massacre. I watched as the 10 outfield players, their six and our four, followed the ball wherever it went like a swarm of bees. My old Deputy Heads advice came storming back. *'Look for a space, knock it into space'.* I imparted this coaching point at the interval and in the second half, instead of our players following the ball, they did just that. The result was that their six outfield players were frequently caught miles away from the ball when it was dinked speculatively into space by one of ours. Within a moment, one of our players would have it in their possession and had a mass of space to run into. Not only that, they had options, as the others dispersed looking for spaces. The game ended 6-0 to us. I was officially a Football Coach. With a little more of the same, and a few more hints, the fabulous five reached the Semi-Final, only to be knocked out by the eventual winners 1-0 in a closely fought game. For some reason I was hero worshipped by other parents, for my insightful coaching and encouragement, which I, modestly accepted.

The lesson here then is about three things; clearly defined roles, being in the correct position and opportunities.

In business we could apply these principles quite easily. Let's look at them one at a time.

If you have someone whose skills are clearly defined and obvious, playing them out of position, or making them play in a position where their strengths are not correctly utilised, is not a great use of resources. It's not just about coaching though it's more of an organisational discipline. Where the coaching comes in is when you look at the way someone is playing or working and see the potential. In other words, a player with a strong right foot playing on the right. Move him to the left and coach him on cutting inside, setting himself at 90 degrees or less to the target and then letting go. In the workplace it may be that you recognise his strength and see that it is misplaced. You might move him to an area alien to him but where that strength can be exploited. The coaching comes in where you suggest the equivalent of 'cutting inside'. It might be, for example that a member of the team is working in a technical role, but is always able to make a positive contribution to the management of project when the guys on the ground doing the installations have a problem. In other words, he is in the wrong place at the right time. The clean strike of the ball is always going to drift and miss the target. Put him on the ground with the installation team and coach him to lead them. It might be that, given the right coaching, he will 'cut inside' and create that space, realise where those teams have had so much trouble in the past and be able to improve the definition of best practice. Bang; top corner, one nil.

Being in this position he now also has a clearly defined and challenging role. Like the footballer, he can cut inside and have a shot himself, or deliver a killer pass right into the danger zone. He can see and read what's going on far more clearly than he could on support and he can interpret signs and signals that there may be impending issues. Before, the modus operandi was largely hit and hope for the best. Now he has targets and a much clearer path. The coaching point here is to let him loose and be allowed to develop. Give him hints and sometimes specific, measurable coaching targets. Such as reducing the installation time or looking at pre-preparing configurations off-site. Bang; bottom corner, two nil.

Which brings us to the third factor, opportunities, i.e. the space in which to play. He now sees and understands all the reasons why he had so many calls for support. He's now had a chance to manage his way through those, first hand. He now understands why we have not been so efficient at installation time. He can see the opportunities for himself and the team to make things more efficient and make savings. A good coach, listening to his report and feedback on the field work, will encourage the team member to take more of a free hand. *'Don't look for someone to pass to or to cross to all the time, go for the goal yourself!'* Bang; three nil!

A pessimist sees the difficulty in every opportunity; an optimist sees the opportunity in every difficulty. Winston Churchill.

Trying ideas out is about experimentation. If they don't work, as long as the person making them happen is skilled and competent, they can back out of them and restore the status quo. Encourage this if you have confidence in your staff to do it, but remember, don't hold them accountable for your misjudgements.

Having discussed putting a person in the right position and letting him find his own space, we come to another point that we touched on earlier; looking for the space. As a coach, you need to have team members or individuals looking for those opportunities. They need to be able to recognise that space and the opportunities that are presented by it. It is at that point, once they can recognise it, that they need the second coaching point and that is 'what to do with that opportunity, how to use that space.'

Let's take an example here. You have a young salesperson visiting a client in the Retail Sector. Your salesperson is selling one of your minor services, a courier swap out of an item of equipment. The terms are next day, like for like swap, configured out of the box.

You may have coached the salesperson to ask a few questions about the wider operation, without being too pushy. The last thing you want to do is look like you have an agenda.

It is not a big deal, they have five hundred of these in several locations, but it is what you may consider to be a foot in the door to a more lucrative deal later. Whilst out on site the salesperson hears from their contact that they are looking to go to tender on a larger deal, a fully managed service on all their mobile computing. This is something that your firm could handle, but your salesperson has been told to play it without being pushy, so he holds back, but makes a note of it to discuss with you later. A few days are lost here, as he leaves it until he is next in the office, believing it to be a potential opening, but not necessarily that critical. Whatever you do now, you will appear desperate for the business, and you may already be too late.

How could your coaching have been better? I'm sure all the Sales Directors and Sales people reading this will know straight away.

The coaching should have been about looking for the space and knocking the ball into it. The space was there, it was that opportunity. If the salesperson didn't have the experience or knowledge to pursue it they could have laid that killer pass off. In terms of the coaching, you should have put it like this.

Go to see them and pitch for the basic service. Play it straight. Ask about their operation and what kind of kit they have under support. If you see any opportunities for anything bigger, don't get too excited, just close at the end of the meeting by giving the contact an idea of our team structure and just as an aside, mention that one of your colleagues had done a similar deal for another company recently. You could then ask if that deal is closed off and if you could get the colleague to give him a call if he is interested.

In other words, look for the space. Knock the ball in there, let your team mate run into that space and pick up the pass. This approach is less likely to cause a strong defence, because the recipient was probably not expecting it. I always prefer sales people who come across like they want to help me because they are interested in what we do, rather than those that you can tell are just focussed on the dollar.

5.3. Be anxious to win

There is a brilliant quote from Admiral Nelson, said of his fellow Admirals, which goes *"I find that they are more afraid of losing than they are anxious to win."*

It seems the Admiral was not only a glass is half full type, but had the right idea when it came to thinking about his team dynamic. He instilled in them that winning was the only acceptable outcome and helped them shed their fear of losing. In sport, we can see this in many different areas. One great recent example in 2012 concerned Tennis star Andy Murray. Andy had been under relentless pressure, as a top four Player and biggest star in British tennis, since 'Tiger' Tim Henman. Whenever he made it to within a sniff of a Grand Slam title, he choked. It wasn't about stamina, or talent, or technical ability. He became more fearful of losing, than he was anxious to win. The public expectation became the driving force behind that fear. To break a hoodoo that had existed for decades became more important to everyone than Andy actually having his own successes. A change of coach, to the formidable Ivan Lendl altered the dynamic. You could see the direction and level of determination had changed and in 2012 Andy bagged Olympic Gold and his first Slam Title.

Murray's game used to be more defensive, relying on his opponent to make mistakes. He has a great tactical brain and naturally counter-attacking style, which is all well and good against most players, but the top three at the time were really something special, and to beat them, particularly over five sets, you had to have more in your arsenal. You needed to take the game to them, be aggressive and take the offensive, you needed to fight for the title and hunt for it. Murray was up against people who made few mistakes and were players who could play aggressively. Lendl had him introduce a more aggressive forehand and powerful backhand returns. When he struck the ball, he was not just making sure he made a return; he was looking for a winner. He used to hit a lot of baseline shots, maintaining the rallies hoping for a mistake from his opponent, now he varies the shots, there is a definite intent. His second serve is also more potent and attacking. These are really quite subtle changes. Without the talent and skill to execute them, Murray would not have been able to adapt. Part of the issue was self-belief too, if you play defensively, waiting for mistakes, is that because you believe that the opponent is somehow better than you? Belief in self plays a huge part in achieving goals. That is why the really top performers are sometimes confident to the point of arrogance.

In training and coaching sessions Lendl has two players hitting balls at Murray, so he has to think faster and more consistently at a higher pace. When faced with a rapid succession of balls he will try to minimise his own errors and improve his concentration. In addition, he is getting Murray to add other, small changes and dimensions to his game.

When I first started work, after a couple of weeks, I was given a member of staff to manage. I had a few weeks earlier been a schoolboy; it was a bit of a shock to the system. The member of staff I was given to manage – let's call him Keith – was a bit of a no-hoper. He had spent the previous two weeks educating me in all the dodges and tricks, designed to avoid work. His legacy was a priceless catalogue of skives which I had squirrelled away in my infallible memory. As a result, he could not get away with any of them ever again. Several years, three I think, amassing his library were now wasted and in tatters.

In some ways, being given Keith to supervise was a great move, for me and him. I was ambitious, relatively intelligent and a quick learner. He was a large block of clay ready to be moulded into something better. I did not fear the challenge of managing a career skiver. To me it was something I was determined to do properly. Obviously I didn't know anything about coaching. I didn't know much about the detail behind the job we were doing, I was still learning, but I did know about people. I knew that you shouldn't write anyone off. Everybody has their triggers. Keith had never been given anything to feel good about, coming from a background where most of his peers were similar and had a similar frame of mind. He had been there three years and never been given any responsibility or credit for anything. As a result, he had resorted to this downward spiral of avoiding actual work as much as possible and, it seems, successive supervisors had tried, unsuccessfully, to draw him out of it. Their take on it had been to shout at him more loudly and give him a succession of official warnings. All I felt I needed to do was to find those triggers and Keith could be just as reliable as anyone else there.

Our friendly bully, the Manager, made it quite clear that, if I couldn't sort Keith out, it would not help my career. No doubt he had fired up those whom had previously tried with those inspirational words. Now, what he hadn't realised about me was that I had learned some years earlier, that to fear failure, was to fail. I didn't fear failure. I just wanted to win, always.

I started slowly at first; just going through the motions of the job. My own standards of work were high and my superiors were frequently commenting on it. I could see that Keith was unimpressed by this. I saw an opportunity. His little section needed some work and I decided to show him how it should look and then let him do the rest. He watched me work with some pleasure, mainly because he wasn't doing it. As I worked I commented on the key coaching points I felt Keith needed, to be able to emulate my brilliance. I let him take over and watched, reminding him of the coaching points I had previously imparted. After a little while I let him take a step back and look at what he'd done. I could see the look of pride on his face as a trace of a smile appeared and, almost, embarrassment. I let him continue and complete the whole section. After a suitable bouquet from me on his efforts, he went for his lunch. Being a quick learner, I went off and found our friendly Manager, who was busy tearing someone a new fundamental orifice. I took him to see the now impressive section which had been Keith's domain for thirty six months. He was suitably impressed, so then I dropped the nuke and told him Keith had done it. He couldn't believe it. He went to find other Supervisors who had previously failed with Keith and showed them the glowing section. They were a little shocked, but not as shocked as Keith when he returned from lunch and the Manager pounced on him like a long lost friend; hand on his shoulder and telling him that he always knew he had it in him and that his work was 'first class'.

This had been the first step in a process that took me just over twelve months, but before I moved on to another greater challenge, Keith was promoted to Senior Sales Assistant. I don't believe he looked back from there.

I think the point here is about your stance when you begin a daunting process or task. If you begin fearful, the fear is likely to hamstring you and make you more likely to fail. Decisions become much harder to make and each milestone is literally a mile high, instead of a natural and logical progression to the goal. Break it all down, take your time and create achievable steps. Almost anything is achievable once you do that.

5.4. Aggression as a tool

Joey Galloway, referring to Head Coach Bill Parcells: "If you can eliminate the yelling and listen to the message, there's a great message there."

At school, we had a particularly good English teacher, who was quite outspoken and, for want of a better expression, very honest with us all. He had, I believe, been in the RAF and from there had gone on to manage a small Supermarket, before deciding he should turn to teaching. It was this rather odd, mixed background which helped him evolve a certain style of teaching that was totally different to any other teacher I had ever encountered. There was also a mixture of bad language and semi-restrained, violence which was almost humorous on occasion. It was though, something we accepted and didn't really complain about. I think we all recognised that, in spite of it all, we were actually learning something from the man and that what we were learning had some value. Strangely, most of these things were actually nothing to do with English.

The one thing I recall about those lessons was his frustration at us all when we were schlepping our way through Shakespeare or some unfathomable Poetry. He would ask questions like 'What is Falstaff actually saying here?' There would be an uneasy silence as thirty people who hadn't really engaged with the prose, racked their brains and searched through the accompanying notes, to see if there were any clues. 'Oh! Come on, you thicko's.' He would cry at a slightly louder and more intimidating volume, still no-one bleated a word. Then he would scan the room, looking for someone who had the faintest possibility of a glint in their eye, indicating they might have a clue. 'Pattinson, what is Falstaff actually saying here?' Not a sound, as Pattinson tried to disappear, head first into the book. Inevitably, it would end in some form of violence, as his frustration boiled over and we battled to understand something which was actually alien to us. Occasionally, someone – sometimes me – would venture a guess at what he was looking for. We'd be wrong of course, but he would at least acknowledge someone had tried; then batter us with the ruler.

So, what is the point of my story?

When he eventually gave us the answer, usually through clenched teeth, we remembered it. Over time, we began to see the way he had arrived at the answers and believe it or not, we were able, by the time the examinations came along, to interpret the text in something close to accuracy. Now, I'm not suggesting that violence, or the threat of it, is a good approach to take; far from it. There were really two points I wanted to make about it though.

Firstly, it was memorable. Here I am over forty years later recounting it like it was yesterday. Secondly, it made me aware that, in a sporting context, there are probably situations where coaches have to be more aggressive and perhaps shout to get their message across.

Take a Boxer, a little punch drunk from several rounds of fighting; sore, ringing in the ears, adrenalin pounding through his brain. How, as a coach, do you get a couple of simple points across, that might save your man from a further pounding? You shout, you repeat the coaching point, over and over again. In that minute of respite between rounds, you batter him mentally with points necessary to his survival.

In business we can't really do the same. Coaching should be almost imperceptible, not a battering. In fact, if you have to bawl someone out and consider it coaching, it is you who have failed. No, the lessons we can learn from my old Teacher and from the Boxing coach are these. (1) Be memorable. (2) Make the point as often as you need to, until it sticks.

There are several ways to be memorable, without the use of violence. In sports coaching, such as swimming, a lot of the technique coaching can be visual. This is where the coach demonstrates the technique from the poolside, which the swimmer is then supposed to emulate in the water. To demonstrate the speed and nature of a front crawl kick, one might rapidly alternate the movement of the index and middle fingers. Or even the whole arms, flexing the hands to show how the feet should behave during the kick. In a business context, this kind of coaching is more difficult, but you might consider that, as a Coach or mentor, you are setting an example all the time. If one of your team, whom you are coaching, is around when you talk with people or when you ask a question in a meeting, they will learn from your approach. You could easily talk to them them afterwards and say something like, 'Now, did you see the way I approached that question?' Or it may even be, quietly, 'When you're dealing with Geoff, always get him to confirm what it is he's going to do, before you finish the discussion.' These are coaching points, demonstrating technique in the same way you might get another Swimmer to demonstrate a stroke or part of a stroke.

What about being memorable though?

It may be advantageous to develop a style all of your own. Add a little something into the delivery of a coaching point that makes it memorable. Maybe an analogy as we discussed earlier, maybe an anecdote. Let us not forget though that this section is about the use of aggression as a tool.

Aggression can be used effectively in coaching if it is used in a role playing situation, as a School Teacher may use it. I think a hint of it in your inflection is not a bad thing if you want to emphasise a particular point. I had an occasion where I had to speak to a supplier on a conference call. I was actually seething with anger at a position they had put me in. They had assured me that some improvements and changes they had made at a site had been completed effectively and had made a positive impact. For my own benefit I went to that site to see the improvements for myself and to collect what, I imagined, would be positive feedback. Instead, it was very clear after a couple of simple questions that the situation had not improved at all.

Unable to see them face to face, at short notice, I decided that my best course of action was to use some controlled aggression.

As the conference call started, I let the person running the call effect their introduction then I interrupted. I used very few words. I was very precise and very sharp in my tone. Here the words you choose are important. Questions you should ask once you have spelled out what you expect are things like *'Is that clear?'* and *'Is anyone in any doubt?'* Having delivered my ultimatum, coldly and calculated, I left the meeting. The impact of those forty seconds was greater than a half hour face to face. Within a few hours I had a complete plan of action by email, setting out how they would rectify the issues at their own expense.

Now, some would argue that this was not coaching. It was some form of ticking off or to use the vernacular 'a bollocking'. I disagree. I would imagine that at half time, in most Premiership dressing rooms up and down the country a similar situation is being played out. It is not emotional and spur of the moment aggression. It is calculated and measured. It is designed to effect an action not rebuke.

Think of a soldier. Here is an individual who has been broken down into component form and rebuilt to do things which in his normal day to day existence he might not even have considered. He has been trained and conditioned and yes, coached, to kill. Well, that's not strictly true, not of all soldiers. He has really been coached to react. The reaction will be dependent upon the situation or command. It has been drilled into him by continual and relentlessly aggressive coaching, so that should it be required, there will be no hesitation in his reaction to a command or an event. It is, to an extent, programmed. If that reaction is to kill or be killed, then the outcome will hopefully be in his favour.

You can use aggression in your coaching, but the only way it should be used is to create aggression in those you are coaching, to enable them to execute their tasks. You should never use it to reprimand or punish. Once you do that, it is you who have failed, not them.

5.5. Misuse of aggression

The first Manager I worked for was a classic abuser of people and power. His language, both verbal and body language was, by any standards confrontational, unacceptable and negatively charged. His idea of coaching was to spend an hour ripping into someone in the vain hope it might shock them into realising, what it was he actually wanted them to do and, how he wanted them to do it.

There are many examples I could quote. Suffice it to say he was unreasonable, a bully, who continually abused his managers and supervisors and backed all this up by exposing them to the fear of losing their jobs. In those days, you could get rid of someone, without too much difficulty, just because you didn't like them and he frequently did. Had he channelled all the energy he discharged negatively into positivity, he could have been a great manager and coach. Unfortunately, there was little chance of that.

The effect that this had on the workforce, his team, was to make the less intelligent team members fashion themselves in his image and the brighter ones the exact opposite. Thus the divide was created.

I suppose I look back on that whole period now as a learning experience. It was an object lesson in how not to manage, motivate or coach people, but at the time it was a living hell.

I have probably learned more from bad managers, over the years, than I have from the good ones. The simple fact is that when you are on the wrong end of the treatment or approach of a bad manager, you should make sure that you don't practice those methods yourself. Some of the managers I have worked for were probably as far removed from coaches as you could ever position yourself and some were just downright obnoxious.

There are several things which, as a manager, you should never do under any circumstances.

Don't Lie – The person you are lying to will undoubtedly find you out at some point or will realise, through observation, that what you have said is false.

Don't compare – Comparisons are odious and we have touched upon them already. You should not compare individuals against each other as everyone is unique.

Don't lose your cool – Stay calm and remain focussed. Remember that a person's failure may be down to your own lack of attention or detail.

I have examples of all of these of course, taken from my chequered career. As far as lying goes I have one very clear example. A manager I reported to had taken a dislike to me because I was quite vocal about some aspects of his behaviour and also his methods. To try to teach me a lesson he withheld 50% of my annual pay increase, on the grounds that my performance was not up to scratch. I challenged this, but no specifics were forthcoming. I raised the matter to the next level, which at the time, due to absences, just happened to be the MD. The MD called us together and I stated my grievance. The manager stated that he had canvassed recipients of my 'service' and found that they were unhappy and made, in his words, some quite horrifying allegations. I asked for examples. I didn't get any as he claimed it was an inappropriate forum. The MD listened and told us both to go off and sort out our differences separately. I immediately spoke with the Area Manager of the sector concerned and asked if any of his team had any complaints about my service or approach. After a day or so, he came back with a very firm answer, none of them were dissatisfied and none had been approached or asked before by anyone. As I suspected, my manager had lied to me and then expanded upon it in front of the MD. I challenged him on it again, this time using the additional information I now had. He was a little ruffled that I seemingly had more senior support and evidence which I could call upon that might do him some damage. After what he called a couple of week's consideration, I had my missing pay rise re-instated. That was not the end of the matter though. Our relationship was damaged and I moved on from his team to another some months after.

Some years later, after this particular manager had left, the same MD came to me one day and recalled the incident. "I knew he was lying, you know." He told me. "How did you know?" I asked. "He was too calm for someone who had been brought into that situation, whereas you were passionate about your position. Had I been put into that situation, I would have been furious if I had been in the right. He was just too calm. Plus, when he had left, I did exactly what you did, I rang the Area Manager. He said to me, 'Well that's a co-incidence, Tony has just asked me the same question.'" This is a great example of how to read people.

Another manager used to compare people all the time, but especially in his monthly catch up, team meetings. There was one guy in the team who had been given a very exciting brief, to come up with labour and cost saving ideas. These could be anything from re-engineering processes to automation. Some of the automation ideas were borrowed straight from his previous employment and were innovative in our industry. Those of us doing the more mundane, bread and butter work were constantly and aggressively compared to this chap and how high profile his contribution was. This was great example of de-motivation, but also a form of bullying. We didn't have the opportunity to make the same impact as he did, no matter how accomplished and talented we had the potential to be. Putting us under that pressure was unfair and destructive.

There are many types of aggression. It is not just about shouting and threatening language. It can be psychological and very calculated. If it is directed to repress, can be defined as an attack or is in some way designed to deny or destroy a part of you – i.e. your confidence, image, status, credibility or opportunities; it is aggression.

5.6. Positive behaviours

When I coached swimming, the majority of the children I coached were in the 6-9 years age range. As such, when the new swimmers first arrived and were presented with a six foot three, grim looking coach, quite a few of them looked uncomfortable. I had to be a gentle giant, but also be able to control the group. It was a bit of a balancing act. I had to do a lot of smiling, which was not something I was noted for, and be very careful with my general body language.

There was also a balance between maintaining discipline in, what could be a dangerous environment and trying to be positive. Sometimes you had to raise your voice to prevent an accident or occurrence, but you had to keep them relatively happy. Even shaking your head or looking exasperated if one of them set off swimming the wrong stroke was a bad thing and of course, being a coach of children on poolside, you were under the spotlight of the parents all the time. They would listen to what you said, how you said it and pick up on any negative body language. Even if you didn't articulate your feelings to their kids, they would do so later and achieve the same net result; negative feedback.

In work it is sometimes harder to maintain a positive outlook if there are elements of work or coaching which are negatively charged. It is far easier to criticise what is wrong, than to celebrate a job well done. People are generally at a loss to say good things about a performance or piece of work in business. If they thought about it though, there are many things you can say and let's not forget, nothing is ever going to be perfect, you can always manage to slip an improvement coaching point in there. Even if what they have done is what was expected, why not tell them 'Great job, just what we wanted!' is a great piece of coaching feedback; it is affirmation. Sometimes, that is just what people are looking for.

Your positive behaviours, as coaches or managers, should be fostered in your people too. If they are approachable, affable, positive and cooperative, people will like dealing with them. They will discuss how good an experience it has been and your team or individuals will be the ones that people want to deal with.

Behaviours, as a leader and as a coach are very important in terms of setting out your stall. If rigid discipline is important to the sport, or the place of work, then as a coach or manager, you must embody that discipline. There is often an element, within this, of setting a minimum standard of behaviour, rather than just repeatedly higher standards of achievement. I worked with a manager who had a drawer full of neckties, which he would supply to external visitors if they arrived without one for a meeting. It was a standard he maintained that if you were attending a business meeting, you should look businesslike. Don't let anyone else cause you to let your own standards slip. This applies equally out of work. If you are the coach or manager, you can let your hair down with everyone else, but set a minimum standard and don't descend below it. You may wonder why it is so important to do this, but it is a fundamental premise of good coaching and a good coach-coachee relationship. If you are a good coach, people will learn not just from your coaching points, targeted and purposeful, but from your body language, seemingly throw-away comments and facial expressions. The people you coach will believe that they are always being observed and will therefore always be scrutinising you. Not because they are trying to catch you out, but because they feel they have to model themselves on you. That minimum standard must therefore be the lowest accepted behaviour you would expect from yourself and those in your charge.

You can't always be there, either as a coach in business or in sport, so the behavioural disciplines for the 'game' or when the employee is working independently of you must be communicated and coached too. Professionalism is a word often abused in this context. Not all professionals behave impeccably and not all amateurs are ill-disciplined, even though that is what it implies. You have to decide what the criteria are for your role and those of your charges and ensure that this model is the one they aspire to when they are, 'in the game'.

Positive behaviour is especially important when things go wrong. You have to keep calm and remember that, *you are where you are*. Being negative at that point will not change that or alter the fact that you may need to implement some form of expedient resolution. Take the team or the individual on a journey, from exactly where you are, to where you need to be. Go through it with them and accept their suggestions, work out a plan and bring them along with you. Always remember that their failure may ultimately be your fault. You can't take credit for their successes if you are not prepared to accept that.

5.7. Keeping something back

Another trait of the particularly bad Manager, I mentioned earlier, was the fact that he was aggressive all the time. His voice, if not raised, mostly resembled a snarl. There was absolutely nothing in the man's character, which could be classed as pleasant. On one occasion, even when he told me he was promoting me, the introduction to that news, was delivered in such a way as to suggest that I might be about to get the sack. It was aggression and angst for its own sake, taken to extremes and whilst memorable, only served to reinforce in my mind how not to manage.

It is basic psychology that a behaviour, which is repeated constantly, becomes the norm. It becomes the accepted, if not the acceptable norm. This is exactly what happened here. Over a period of time, all the members of staff, supervisors and managers who served under him knew of no different way for him to behave. As a consequence, there was no way for him to articulate the difference between a normal everyday bawling out and a genuine crisis bawling out. There was no higher gear to slip into, no extra burst of pace available, no harder punch to throw. In that way, his confrontational and aggressive management style had severely limited him and also weakened him. Short of pleading with people – which I suspect would not have been on his list of plausible options – there was nothing else he could do when it came to a real problem.

A manager, who came to work under him at the time, offered a totally different view. Harvey was a witty, well educated and down to earth guy, who believed that the workplace should be an abode you enjoyed being in. He made it his quest to form a barrier between the fire breathing ogre and the rest of us and to develop in all of us, a better way of thinking about the way we managed people. The two styles were diametrically opposed. A typical example might be.

Bad manager - "Get that done NOW!" Usually with an appropriate (or inappropriate) expletive thrown in for good measure.

Harvey - "Try and quicken it up a bit mate."

It was the same message, with the same ultimate goal, but delivered in a totally different style. One is direct, aggressive and at a command level, the other is a request in a friendly but urgent tone, like there is a genuine reason for working a bit quicker. Also, Harvey restrained, for as long as was humanly possible, any aggression or even a hint of aggression. He only once, to my recollection, lost his temper and shouted at someone and it was such a shock, such a rare occurrence, that the individual it was aimed at sprang into action. To me this proved that, it wasn't the aggression that had become an established norm, but the fact that a particular individual practiced it. When Harvey used it, it had far more impact and people realised that there was a real issue to be dealt with.

In coaching, you should always keep something in reserve. If you don't, you will quickly run out of options. Remember what we said earlier about the Golf coach, sending us off round the course with a seven iron and a putter. We learned to work with a limited set of resources. It taught us to develop a more skilful touch and vary the use of power. You could argue that, limiting yourself to a particular level of urgency, in most situations, would be desirable, so that you have other more powerful tools and resources in reserve.

We had a Director who was a master in the use of sarcasm. It was, generally quite amusing, unless you were the direct recipient of it. Then it was quite clearly a warning shot. Example: When faced with a particularly high customer display, he was heard to say, "We expecting a visit from the Watutsi tribe then?" The Watutsi being a tribe from Africa whose average height is supposed to exceed seven feet. The sarcasm was not lost on the unfortunate Manager who it was aimed at, and he knew he had better sort it out quickly. There was no aggression, no malice or threat in the quip. It was a good style. It was memorable; it was repeated in folklore and feared by others as word spread. They didn't want to hear anything like that aimed at them. The Director knew that, if he could get people to respond using his wit, like that, the big guns could be saved for when they were really needed. Apparently, although I never saw it myself, those big guns were awesome.

Not having the world's greatest wit and an appalling sense of humour, I always try to be conciliatory and helpful with my initial criticisms. If I need to escalate the criticism, it will become a firm suggestion that the piece of work should be done in a particular way. The next level is a very short, not aggressive but rather direct approach, with an economy of words. There are other levels available, such as shouting and more aggressive behaviour, but I regard those as a personal failure.

To use a sporting analogy again, if you used the driver, hit at full tilt, for all your golf shots, you would very rarely, if ever, reach par. There is a fine old quote, 'Power is nothing without control'. It is very true and should be applied to behaviours and the use of aggression in coaching. Always keep something back.

The most effective use of keeping something back was also executed by another former Director. He would invite you to use his eyes. Now this seems a strange concept, but consider. If you use few words to convey when you are unhappy or feel that there could be an improvement. You are actually getting the person to identify what needs attention themselves. His modus operandi was to walk at a steady pace up and down the workspace, looking at displays and in utter silence. When he found something he didn't like, he lingered just a fraction longer, looking at whatever it was then, he would move on. The hapless manager following would have to quickly look and spot what he had seen, either fix it or make a note to fix it, before catching him up again. At the end of his tour, he would go off and have a cup of coffee, then return and make the same tour. Now, as a Manager, what you wanted here was a clear round, with no faults. You did not want him hesitating at a fence, especially one you had seen him hesitate at once before.

In the business context, it was very effective. The Manager gradually learned what sort of things the Director was identifying and, prior to his visits, would walk the floor himself looking with the Directors eyes. The high point being one Saturday, when he arrived, walked the whole floor and strolled out again without a word. As a coach, he had just seen us win Olympic gold. More importantly, he had coached us all, without having done anything other than to get us to use our own eyes, knowledge and experience.

I couldn't finish this short section without identifying how that approach might work in sport. Many teams or individuals watch film of themselves in action, to see what they are doing wrong and more importantly, what they are doing right. One terrific example was Swimmer Mark Foster, who used cameras to film himself in a free flow pool. This is a pool where the swimmer actually swims against a current to stay in the same place, whilst the water flows over them. Tracking a swimmer with cameras has always been difficult, for a variety of reasons. This method allowed Foster to examine his position in the water and elements of his stroke and technique that he and his coach hadn't previously been able to see. As a result, he realised that for the pull part of his stroke, his arm wasn't close enough to his body, which was creating too much body roll and affecting his shape in the water.

There are people who take the 80/20 rule to its extreme. I'm referring to those who spend 80% of their time publicising what they have done and only 20% of the time actually making a contribution. They will dress up and embellish what they have done, making sure that everyone right up to the CEO knows about it, when really the contribution they are making is not that important. This type of individual will also look for opportunities to enhance their standing, even if that means grinding someone into the ground with their heel on the way. I am of course talking about the 'workplace politicians'. Everyone has to play a little politics now and then to get by. It is not pleasant and not everyone is good at it, but it does, unfortunately, happen. On the flip side, there are those whose entire existence is supported by their political stance. If they see an opportunity to demean someone else, criticise them or their work, whilst at the same time, enhancing their own status, they will take it. They will also say things like "We have to be seen to be doing......." Why not just do?

I don't mention the office politicians because they have a part to play in coaching. On the contrary, I mention them because a) they have no place in coaching, and b) you should coach your people so that they insure against anyone with any political motivations. It is not an easy thing to do. With some of the more skilled operatives, you can never be quite sure which direction they are going to take. I have seen many examples, here are just a couple to give you a flavour.

A colleague was working closely with a service provider and discovered a bug in a third party program. Quite rightly, he informed the key stakeholder of the issue and kept them informed regularly on progress until root cause was identified and a fix was being hastily pulled together. In the meantime, the stakeholder had requested a meeting with his Director and asked why their team had to find such a fault and bring it to our attention. No mention that my colleague and the Service Provider had alerted *them* to the issue. No mention of the regular communication which had taken place between them.

On another occasion, another colleague had recommended a course of action to solve a particular recurring issue. The stake holder's team, who were notorious glory seekers, distanced themselves from the solution and made verbal statements of opposition. The solution was approved, implemented and solved the issue, at which point the stake holder team produced a report to their Director a statement that, working with I.T., they had come up with a solution to the problem.

Both of these issues seem fairly innocuous, by themselves, but this is the kind of thing that can go on daily, undermining the value of the work your team does.

So how could you coach your people to defend against this sort of approach? In the first one, it is quite simple. The resolving team had not included their Director in the initial emails and regular Communications. Had they done so, they would have prevented the 'distortion of the truth' which came later.

In the second case, again the implementing team should have sought written clarification that the stakeholder was not happy with the proposal.

Both of these may seem like *they* are political and exercises in covering your back, but you have to coach your people to be politically savvy, if not overtly political themselves. It is the only way that they will learn how to look at a situation and ask themselves what possible political capital could be made out of what they are doing, by anyone else.

In all cases, the business politicians are all about influencing thinking and decision making, but without having to do any hard work. You may be wondering where the sporting analogy comes in here. Quite simply, when someone makes a plea for out in cricket, when they are convinced it wasn't; when a footballer raises his hand to get the throw or corner, when he knows he took the last touch, these are all examples of politics at work.

The skill you impart to your team in *keeping their powder dry* or having a trump card, just in case, is one which they will thank you for. In sport, it's that surprising shot that no-one expected, or a tactic no-one has predicted. In business it's about looking at the job, the dynamics of those involved, what might happen and then preparing for it; that's all. It's not playing politics, if that is something you abhor, it is being aware of politics and taking mitigating action against it.

In Chapter five we have explored the artistic side of our approach, but with the science firmly in mind. Elements such as first touch and seeking out opportunities are important, but the positive use of tools such as aggression and a desire to win, rather than a fear of failure are equally vital. We have looked at different types of aggression and how and when they can be used. We have also looked at establishing norms and in doing so, highlighting the contrast when you need to do something different to affect a result. We have also briefly touched upon politics. Why it is important to coach awareness of it, rather than be a practitioner of it and how to manage your way through the minefield of business politics. In the final chapter, we will look at the relationships you should focus on in your coaching. With those you coach, but also, with yourself.

CHAPTER 6.
ME, YOU AND THEM

In this final chapter we look at the most important aspect of coaching, me you and them. The relationship we have with our charges, the people we coach in business or in sport, is the most significant aspect to the whole topic. So you may ask why I have left it until the last. Why didn't I talk about that first, then everything else would be easier? Well, I don't believe it would.

The previous chapters have dealt with the aspects of coaching which are all pretty much the same, wherever you go. People though, are not and neither are you, neither am I. We are all individuals, with our own motivations, problems, neurosis, fears, difficulties, in short, our own lives. What has made and shaped us to be what we are is a set of unique circumstances, situations and interactions with other equally unique people.

So, having learned the good things about coaching and what things to avoid, we now come to the tricky bit. To be a great coach, even to be a good coach, you have to understand yourself, the people whom you are coaching and you have to be able to adapt what you have learned to deal with those differences. Now, if we hadn't learned those things already, we couldn't really start to adapt them, could we? So in the following sections, we will learn how to get to understand people, including ourselves and how to really get the best out of them.

Equally, if it is important for us as coaches to understand ourselves, then we need to get our people to understand their selves. Remember coaching is about independence. If you can reach a point where your people carry the coaching with them and use it, you will have succeeded.

You also need to be able to coach them in the importance of trying things out. If you never try anything, you will never achieve anything. Having that confidence and belief in your abilities is a great thing to impart. It is not simply about telling someone they are great, it is about getting them to demonstrate that to themselves. Generally, the more talented someone is, the more self-critical they can be. That is not a bad thing as long as they maintain their self-belief and they use the critique to positive effect. That self-belief is very important to developing greatness.

6.1. The first resort of the lazy person

Paul Richards: "Tell a ballplayer something a thousand times, then tell him again, because that may be the time he'll understand something."

I also quote from my own work of fiction here. A little known and even less read work than this, entitled 'Stand Still, Don't Move'. The quote is that *'The first resort of the lazy person is to let someone else do their thinking.'* If you think about it, there can be no lazier practice. It's not as if you have to get out of your chair and do anything physical, or even attempt something difficult, like speaking to a colleague, and yet there are hoards of people in business, working for companies like yours, who don't use their brains. What's worse is that we, as managers, let them do it. You may believe right now that you don't, *'not me!'* Think about it, you will have done so quite recently. In the day to day rumble that is our working day, someone will ask us a question. It might be a simple as, *'Who does this document need to go to now?'* So without thinking too deeply, you rap the answer back. They go away happy and you try to resume the train of thought that was interrupted. Now, let's rewind a moment. The person who asked you that question has done that particular job before, and asked the very same question before, a couple of times. They have in effect, borrowed your brain to find the answer, rather than try and remember. I find this utterly lazy and almost criminal, to the point of abuse.

People will always ask questions, for reassurance, because they genuinely can't remember, or because the initial training they had wasn't adequate. To continually ask the same question, because they are too lazy to think, is quite different. You need to be aware of these things as a coach and manage it effectively. If you were continually reminding a Golfer or a Swimmer of some fundamental part of the stroke or technique, you would begin to look for another way of putting it across. So why do we tolerate it in our workplace? For expediency; it is easier to actually give the answer, and faster, than to stop, deliberate, dissect and give a coaching point.

Whilst it might be expedient at the time, this is something which will grow if not unchecked. If someone can't be bothered to remember simple things, what are they going to be like with more complicated issues or with something you have trusted them to do?

I was once in this position with a member of staff, whom I had diligently trained to administrate a trading system. They had several stages to go through, to put a new supplier on the test system, make several test transmissions in both directions then put them on the live system. Being a former trainer, I had a certain amount of skill in disseminating the tasks and making it crystal clear what was required, including knocking up my own training notes, with screen shots. There was a point though, after a week or two, where the number of times a few particular questions had been asked, exceeded what was either acceptable or what one might consider normal. I don't know about you, but if I'm finding a particular aspect of something hard to grasp, I'll make my own notes and work through them a couple of times. Not this person. This was a genuine case of running in neutral, whilst the boss did all the thinking. Having gone through the processes where they were encountering the difficulty a couple of times, I began to lose my patience. I sat and thought about my possible alternatives.

1) I could shout at them and tell them to get a grip.
2) I could re-train them. Going through it all again.
3) I could blame my own training methods and skills and try and do it differently.
4) I could coach them.

In the end, having choked down my frustration, I decided to use coaching. The big question was what form should that take? The problem was not about their ability to complete the task, it was about their willingness to actually think about the task and execute it, without first asking once again, how to do it.

I decided that the problem was not related to the task, but to the individual. I thought about how I would tackle a similar situation in my sports coaching. I would have used analogies, examples and a demonstration by someone else. This was, though, different. They knew *how* to do it. They just didn't think about it first.

In the end, I asked them to write down, in their own words, the entire end to end process of that particular task, leaving nothing out. They asked why. I said it was to gain an understanding of how effective my training had been. They seemed quite happy at that, believing that I was preparing to beat myself up for being a lousy trainer. I can remember doing a similar thing coaching a swimmer. I asked them to show me, what I had just shown them, for the umpteenth time. They did it faultlessly.

So here, on the contrary, I was making quite a subtle point. They would have to think. They would have to go through the process, step by step and have to disseminate exactly what they were doing and how they were doing it. After a day or so, the written document appeared. It was proudly presented on four sides of A4, split into sections. I read through it and found only one small semantic error, which I ignored. Technically it was accurate, if not as eloquent and descriptive as my training guide.

The point was that all the questions they had ever asked were answered in that Tome. The answers to questions that had been repeated and repeated were clearly set out in some detail. I smiled to myself. I went back with some really positive feedback. *'I tell you what. You really know your stuff!'* I said, with some admiration in my tone. It had the desired effect. A couple of days later, I almost swallowed my tongue. The party caught my attention and started a sentence *'Tony, you know when you....'* I froze for a second, believing I was about to be asked one of the perennial questions, but they continued *'Oh, no, It's okay, I know what it is.'* I was never asked any such questions again.

Napoleon "Nothing is more difficult, and therefore more precious, than to be able to decide."

This is just one example, it is quite a good one, but there are those where decision makers always defer to you. They are not always looking for reassurance, but for you to make their decision for them. A good coach will turn it around. They will talk it through with the party concerned. A typical dialogue might go like this:

Staff Member – I'm not quite sure what to do about the problem at Rainford.
Coach/Manager - What is making you unsure?
Staff Member – I don't know really, I can't quite put my finger on it.

Now, what they are doing is trying to get you to go through the facts and figures or the problem and make the decision for them. Stop. Think like a Sports coach. At this point you should get them to go through the facts again and come up with a few suggestions, which you could both then go through. What and how you coach after that will depend on what they come back with, but you should be able to pick out the correct solution, one that you would have picked, and steer them to making the decision, without doing it for them.

A runner knows that their strength is waiting in the pack until the last 2km of a 10km race then kicking out for the finish. A race is coming up where two of their rivals, who also have the same kind of strengths are competing and you are waiting for them to decide how they might run it. Your knowledge tells you that your runner, previously a 1500m runner, can go earlier if they want to, but they seem reluctant to make that call themselves. They know the details, of course they do. Sports people are absolutely tuned in on the competition. It is the decision making they can be lazy about. As a coach, your best course of action is to get them to talk you through how the race might go, lap by lap. At some point, you will get to the decision points. Get them to talk through the possible scenarios depending upon the decision they make. The answer will be obvious and they will have chosen their strategy. Next time, they might just do that in their head first.

Let's go back to our team member then. Make them talk through the problem and the possible solutions. When you get to the decision points, don't offer any advice, just take it in. Ask questions like; *'So what if you did this.....?'* Get them to tell you, what they think the outcome would be. If this process is repeated, they will gradually realise that they are getting to the correct decision themselves, just by you prompting them with well chosen questions. There will come that magic point when they actually ask themselves those questions, without asking you first. Then you have done a good job.

When a sportsman goes out on the field, course, or into a race, they are essentially on their own. This is when the true power of the coaching comes in. Can they remember and execute the things you have brought out of them, under pressure and in the game? In business, it may be slightly different, because they can call a timeout and ask for advice, but the true quality of your coaching is when they don't do that, perhaps only letting you know what they are going to do or even better, what they have done. The level of confidence a person can reach, when they can make a decision for themselves is awesome. This is where you will really see a person develop.

6.2. Understand yourself

There is an old saying, probably from the Bible, which goes something like, 'Don't try to remove the splinter from a friend's eye, before you have taken the log from your own.' In other words, sort yourself out, before you advise others. That is very good advice and to a Coach, an absolute necessity.

I recall as a relatively new coach, being in a position where I found myself coaching a higher group than I was used to. These young children, probably 10-11 years old, knew that I normally coached a younger and less experienced group and assumed that I wasn't qualified to coach them. They perhaps thought that I lacked the technical knowledge and couldn't really help them move forward. I could sense a sort of contempt in the way they looked at me and the way they answered simple questions. I made a mistake right away. I asked them what sort of warm up they normally did. Every suspicion, they might have had, was immediately confirmed. I didn't know what I was doing.

This, they believed, gave them the right to question and correct what I might ask them to do next. 'We normally start with freestyle.' They said, when I announced we were going to do 4 x 100 Fly off a ninety second rotation. It was a battle from then on, to get the session back on track and restore discipline. If I corrected something in a swimmers stroke, you could see that it was advice taken with a 'pinch of salt'. I stayed calm though. To lose it at that point and either shout or remind them who the coach was would have been fatal. As they set off on a sixteen length front crawl swim, I began to think about my approach and what I had done wrong. I had exposed myself to them as a novice even though, in technical understanding and qualifications, I wasn't and they had then decided, without any conferring, to treat me with contempt. Why had I asked them that stupid question at the start? Why hadn't I prepared properly? There was little point in me trying to dislodge the odd splinter from their eyes, whilst I stood on poolside with a Canadian Log cabin in mine. Needless to say, that this session was a washout. There was no way I could recover from it. I had one last throw of the dice by making their warm down, or contrasting activity, memorable, I decided to set up some team relays. They went away having enjoyed that part of the session, buzzing with adrenalin.

The key learning for me from that session was to put it behind me. I then did my homework and wrote a coaching plan for the next session, which was challenging from the word go and was absolutely targeted at the things I had witnessed in the previous session. As they began to arrive and get ready for the warm up, I stayed quiet and contemplative. Once they were all assembled I rapped out the instruction for the warm up, no hesitation, no questions; no pleasantries. They set themselves off at five second intervals, as was the norm. These were disciplined swimmers. The rest of the session was equally disciplined and like clockwork. I noticed during some of the exercises, that a couple of the more vocal ones from the previous sessions were shooting each other glances. Their expressions could be read quite clearly. 'This guy *does* know what he's doing.' 'This is hard, but I'm enjoying it,' and other similar inferences. At the end, they were asking if I would be coaching them for the next session. They had, without exception, taken on every tip, hint and coaching point I had passed on. So what was different? Simple; I didn't lack confidence this time. I was in control, prepared and decisive.

This is just one example; a fairly innocuous one too. You can take it much further. You cannot preach to a member of a team, or an individual if you are in any way guilty of the very thing you are preaching about. In this case, I had started off loose and seemingly not knowing my own mind. The Swimmers behaved in exactly the same way. It is no good either, playing the 'I know, because we're very alike,' card. That is crass stupidity and very naive. Imagine trying to stop someone exhibiting a particular behaviour, by telling them it's wrong and you know this, because you do it. No coach is whiter than white, just as no person is. However, as far as coaching is concerned, you must be free of the things you want your managers or athletes to be free of.

In the world of work, I once worked under a manager who was frequently criticised by his peers for his dress sense. I believe that his aim was to appear unique. For example, I once saw him wear a three piece bottle green suit, with a bright yellow shirt and a red and cream patterned wool tie. It was quite a combination. All of this would have been acceptable and passed off as mildly eccentric, had it not been for the fact that, in one of my appraisals, he criticised something I had once worn! Now, you might find that amusing. I know I do looking back; but the point is that his credibility was from then on as suspect as his dodgy dress sense. One of his other classics was to observe me delivering a session to a couple of members of staff at one of the Company locations in a cramped office, After the two hour session he criticised me for standing up through the entire thing. The fact that there were only three chairs, and no more space for a fourth, bypassed him completely.

Earlier in my career, I had encountered a very inexperienced manager, who had come to us from a smaller competitor. He exhibited the traits I had shown in my first coaching session with the swimming group. Though, he lacked knowledge, control and skill, he also had a very weak personality and frequently caved in when his judgement was questioned. The net result of this was that the job got done in spite of him, not because of him, but there was no development, no improvement. In some businesses, if you don't continually improve, you will effectively go backwards. Ultimately, it was evident that his position was untenable. The big mistake he made, having been put in a position where he was, effectively, out of his depth, was not to take stock and learn from those already there doing the job. He had the authority by dint of his position. He could have winged it long enough to get a foot-hold; instead he came in guns blazing and looked a fool.

There are very clear boundaries you should establish as a coach in business, that apply equally to those in sport. 'Do as I say, not as I do,' is not one of them. As a coach you have to be a teacher, a mentor, a role model and a confidant. If you fail on any one of these, you will lose credibility and the confidence of your charges.

You must know yourself to be able to achieve this. You must understand what motivates you and what guides you. You must analyse everything you do in a coaching session and assess the impact and the consequences.

Here is a very important point. The steps you make in coaching, those little chips with the chisel we spoke of earlier, are like the careful placing of dominoes. You will have seen these intricate patterns placed, so that when the first domino is tipped, it will execute a sequence, each one gently tapping and knocking over the next. A 'domino' placed now, may not fall for some years, but the fact that it has been put in place, is fundamental to the whole sequence working. Even one mistake could mean that later, that pattern stops. Think of your behaviour, your attitude and your disposition as a coach, even the words you use, to articulate a view, as those dominoes. Place them carefully and understand the cause and effect that even tiny inputs can make.

You must also decide what type of coach you are. Ask yourself three questions:

1. Under what circumstances do I coach best?
2. How do I respond to being coached?
3. How often do I admit I am wrong?

The answers should help you come up with guidance parameters for yourself on how and when you should coach. Let's examine each one to see what benefit there is in the analysis.

Under what circumstances do I coach best?

There may be times when you are at your best when coaching, there will be times when you should avoid it. For example, if you have just had a rough journey or some bad news. You can't just turn up and begin coaching effectively, you have to prepare. Know what affects your coaching adversely and make sure that you iron those situations out. Know what kind of things put that spring in your step and a twinkle in your eye. A happy coach means that the coachee will probably enjoy the coaching more.

How do I respond to being coached?

This might seem irrelevant in terms of coaching others, but it does have a very strong bearing. You may not like being obviously coached. You may want to be coached systematically, you may find some coaching patronising. Only by knowing these things and how they make *you* feel, will you be able to judge how your charges might feel.

How often do I admit I am wrong?

Now, no-one is infallible. Pretending you are always right or not admitting when you have erred is not a great trait. Whenever you offer a coaching point that doesn't play out in the job or the sport, you were wrong and you need to admit it and move on. If you try and come across as someone who is always right (even when they are clearly wrong), your credibility as a coach will be undermined.

There is one other major difference between the way we coach in business and the way that sports coaching is executed, particularly at professional or World Class level. This is mainly because coaching in business is relatively immature and is only just beginning to gather any sort of momentum and also because significant changes in the way in which sport is approached professionally have really only begun to take root in the last 15-20 years. Business is playing catch up and the process of learning from Sport is slow. Unless you have been there yourself, as a coach, or have had the revelation revealed to you, it will not become obvious.

If you think about many of the examples we have already discussed, they are largely interactions between the team or individual and the coach. We must not forget that in sport, there is usually a backroom staff behind the team or the individual, being part of the support team, training or medical specialists or looking after aspects of development. A professional Soccer team for example may have the following backroom staff, supporting the team and the coaches' efforts.

- Statistical and DVD analysis – Will analyse player performance such as distance covered, passes made, tackles made, shots on goal, fouls etc.
- Logistics – Will organise travel, accommodation for the team and support staff.
- Sports medicine – A generalist who will look at the whole spectrum of medical fitness.
- Physiotherapist – Specific physiotherapist.
- Massage Physiotherapist – Specific massage physiotherapist.
- Psychologist – Without stating the obvious, a brain physiotherapist
- Strength and Conditioning trainer – This is becoming much specialised and has its roots in sports science.
- Team Selectors – Those that will help the team Coach pick the team and substitutes.
- Kit/Equipment – A team who will ensure the team have all the kit they need to wear/use in the execution of the sport and the training.
- Sponsor – Someone who is a stakeholder in the team and has a financial investment in it.

Let's not forget that this is just one example and other teams may have more or less of those in the backroom. Let us also not forget that an individual sportsperson could have a team like that looking after them; a Tennis star, Golf Professional or even a sprinter. It is quite amazing that sport provides us with this excellent and diverse support model, when generally business provides us, by comparison, with a best endeavours approach.

Clearly in a business context, you would not necessarily need all those roles supporting your team, and indeed, the coach – you as a manager – would undertake some of them, probably without thinking about it. I would think that you could come up with a list of specialist roles you might employ, if you had the budget and resources to do it.

- Career and development advice
- Policy and legal advice
- Financial advice
- Human Resources
- Social Advice
- Physical fitness/health advice

There is a common thread running through these and it is quite plain to see if you work in a large or advanced organisation. Most of these functions are now undertaken, to an extent, by HR departments. Caring organisations may also have schemes to provide financial and health advice. As a coach, do not ignore these resources if they are available to you. People, generally, only turn to Human Resources when they have a problem or want to discipline an employee. You should again think about the positive elements they can provide, perhaps to a greater degree than you could ever hope to deliver, and use them to help your charges improve their roles, their careers and their working conditions. Think about it; if an employee has financial or health concerns, they are bound to bring those worries to the workplace. This will distract them from doing a good job. The career and development advice should tie in to the skills matrix and the role profiling you have already undertaken, either in your own team or as an organisation. Along with your HR advisors you can map out a plan for those with potential and ensure that they know and agree what their talents and core skills are and where they might be best used.

All of which neatly leads us on to another key point in terms of our role as coaches. We have already touched upon it to a degree. It is about the position you are prepared to take, in relation to the people you are coaching. If you look at both of the above lists of support personnel, in Sport and in Business, they are there to provide a service to the coach and to the Coaches team or individual. They and the Coach are, in effect, providing a service to those being coached. You might argue with that, you might strongly disagree, but just for a moment, think about the role you have.

As a sports coach, you have a team or an individual who is, probably, more capable than you, has greater potential than you in the sport and by raising their game/standard, it will improve your standing as a coach. In business, a similar thing applies. In your teams, you are providing a service to the colleagues you manage. If you don't provide that service, they will not achieve, improve or complete the work on your behalf.

You have to accept and understand that, as far as the people you are coaching are concerned, they are more important than you. Whether you are more senior in Business terms, or have won more trophies as a coach, than they are ever likely to, is irrelevant. Their welfare, state of mind, working environment, development and ultimately benefits are all aspects of your fundamental obligation to them and a very important part of your role.

6.3. Getting them to understand themselves

As a species we are great at looking outwards and criticising what we see. We can see the failures and weaknesses in others and are not afraid to comment on them. What we are not very good at, is looking inwards with the same critical eye. We have already covered what we should do to look at and understand ourselves better, but how do we coach people to do the same? It is not just about performance or results it is about disposition, behaviours and perception. We might be well motivated as coaches to look inwardly, so that we can look outwardly more effectively, but what is in it for the people we coach to do the same?

A footballer who is hard in the tackle and uncompromising will get a reputation for it. It can become a curse, because the referees will be watching for the crunching tackle, no matter how fair it may be, and be ready to penalise it. Take the example from the 1970's in Britain of the Leeds United player, Norman Hunter. Norman was not a shrinking violet in his competitiveness. He was a tough guy in a tough team and he let the opposition know who was boss. So much so that the crowd carried banners such as 'Norman bites yer legs'. This was unfortunate, because it quickly became his nickname. There were and still are players who are as hard in the tackle and as uncompromising as Norman, but they have adopted a level of subtlety with it, so that they are barely noted for being aggressive. It's a little like the difference between a hammer and a nail gun. Both achieve the same thing, one with a number of loud bangs and a lot of arm waving, the other with nothing more than the sharp hiss of the compressor.

In a number of sports, there are characters that have an image or personae that they have developed in parallel with their skills. Whether that is down to the coach or to the player themselves is debatable. Take Tennis star Andy Murray again. We have already discussed Andy in his struggle to find the right coach. Andy had focussed his entire energies on developing his skills and varied shot repertoire, and boy did he do a great job. However, people did not warm to the British number one, because of his dour personality. On the court Andy was often angry with himself and critical if he got a shot wrong, it was his way of dealing with it. Off court, he was considered a little boring and even Anti-English, because of one quip about a football match, taken out of context. When Andy finally shook the monkey off his back and made a Wimbledon final, the emotion he showed; those tears he shed after losing to Federer, actually made people warm to him. He then went on to win Olympic Gold and then the US Open (his first slam). Did that change of heart by the public actually help him become more successful?

In business, we can and must coach people to look inwardly and more closely and at the way they portray themselves. How they are perceived can have a bearing on the way they are dealt with by others and the expectation they set when working on a particular job.

Get them to tell you how they feel they come across; correct them if necessary and then find out how they want to come across generally and in specific situations. Ask them how they think they might achieve that.

You should take time with the people you coach to help them understand how they respond to coaching, how they take criticism and what motivates and de-motivates them. If they don't respond well to coaching, you may need to explain to them what your coaching is designed to do. Some people can be very sensitive and even a positive comment, couched carelessly may come across to them in a negative way.

Feedback is all important here in developing the way people understand themselves. If someone has reacted badly in a meeting or to a particular piece of news, don't just leave it and believe that they have learned something. Discuss it and give them some idea of how they might have been perceived. For example, on learning that a piece of work had to be cancelled because an engineer didn't turn up at the site, your team member might blow up in a fit of rage and anger, ready to tear someone to pieces; not just for the lack of engineer (who may have had a valid reason for not being there), but for the lack of communication. The rage may have been disproportionate to the incident and this might be perceived by observers as immaturity, lack of self-discipline or just instability. Your man may just have been trying to express how concerned he was; to show people he cared about the job, perhaps even executing a little role playing. Explain that to him and perhaps ask him to suggest how he might have played it if he wanted to appear calm, in control and decisive. Perhaps you could ask how he might have played it if he wanted to come across as unflappable, pragmatic and a quick thinker. There are any number of combinations, all of which would have been better, image wise, than Mr Angry and petulant.

You may even advocate different approaches, depending upon the circumstances and target audience. In a group meeting of his peers, it may be that he wants to stand out. In this instance you might advocate staying quiet and listening before he says anything. That way it will have more impact when he does and he will appear thoughtful and considered, rather than just someone who desperately wants to be heard. In a project meeting with suppliers and specialists, you might suggest that he takes control and directs the flow of the meeting, coming across knowledgeable, confident and in charge.

I had a chat with one of our MD's some years back. I was frustrated that I hadn't made more progress up the career ladder and, in spite of my achievements it didn't look as if progression was something people were keen to offer me. He advised me to go and talk to a few people about the way I came across. How they viewed me and the impression I gave. I'll summarise the comments I received from senior people, Directors and 'Heads Of'.

You come across as a smart Alec.
You don't seem to have any passion.
You don't stride confidently.
You're too clever, clever for your own good.
You are too fond of a rumour.

There were others, but a few of these hit home quite hard. I had thought, for example, that knowing your stuff and making sure others knew that you did was a good thing. It probably is, but I must have been over emphasising it. I had always thought that to show your emotions (passion) was a sign of weakness. I must not have understood the subtle difference. It hurt a bit to think that, all my good work was undone by how I projected myself, and that I couldn't see it. A very useful and life changing exercise and one I never regret.

6.4. Specialise or generalise

There is a point with swimmers, where their skill is assessed across the range of strokes and their coach may advise them to focus on one particular stroke. They may focus on two, three or all four of the competitive strokes, but usually one or two is the norm. The point at which that transition happens does vary, but it tends to be at the stage where the swimmers are beginning to compete at higher levels, beginning to use ground based training, conditioning and such and recognising where their aquatic skills are really at their best.

In business too, an employee will reach that point. If they are in a technical role, perhaps one covering many facets, they may have a particular talent or skill, which they feel they should concentrate on. It might be that you actually suggest that they specialise, to make best use of their talents, after that it is down to you and them to exploit that decision.

In sport, once that decision is made, the whole focus of the training and coaching, the conditioning and goals will be changed to apply the right flavour to the whole thing. In business, you should do the same.

Equally, if someone is to generalise, in business that usually means that they have designs on management. In sport, they are an 'all rounder'. Here is where things differ slightly. If you have a Michael Phelps or Ian Thorpe, who are brilliant at all of the competitive strokes, they are simply superstars. In business, the equivalent is not necessarily a superstar, but someone with the ability to be a general or professional manager. They know enough about the whole operation to guide and direct it, in a structured and competent manner. They may not wish to specialise, as that will restrict them. They may have sufficient interest in the whole operation to not want to divorce themselves from parts of it.

Once they have made that decision, your coaching should begin to bring them on in all areas and to raise their game either by training courses, coaching and additional responsibility.

Management and Graduate training programmes in larger businesses tend to take the generalist approach. You will find that companies and corporate businesses with long established schemes of this kind have people at Board level who have taken that very route. The success of these schemes is about broad exposure to all areas of the business and at a level which allows them to discover exactly who they are and what their capabilities are. They are in essence management apprenticeship schemes. Just as you will find apprenticeship schemes for technical people, skilled people and trades, these schemes encourage and develop management thinking and a management approach. These managers become adaptable and 'professional' in the sense that they can manage in many different situations and areas.

No matter who they are, or what level they attain, they will still need to be coached. All that changes is the level at which the coaching is done and whether it is specific or general.

If you maintain the talent and skills matrices we mentioned earlier and use the T.A.S.K. analysis to help nurture individuals, you will have a better view of the path they will be best suited to take. I have seen first-hand what happens when a deeply technical person is put into a management role. They generally get bogged down with the technical aspects of their job – their comfort zone – and the soft skills, coaching, people skills, administration and the like are either neglected or seen as an evil they have to endure. This is not a good basis for leading a team when you bear in mind they take their lead from you.

Similarly, trying to make a good generalist occupy a technical role will ultimately end in failure. A good generalist, who has the potential to make a good manager, will understand what it is they need to know about the technical role, but will not deep dive to the extent that they will lose sight of the bigger picture. It is not something they will feel comfortable with.

In sport, consider the goalkeeper in association football. He has very technical skills as a shot stopper. His positioning is key in set pieces and how he manages his defence. He can kick the ball a long way, with some accuracy, both from a drop kick or punt and from a dead ball position, but don't ask him to dribble, or run with the ball, or head it. Very few goalkeepers have any of those skills.

If you look at someone with an obvious ability, don't simply assume that the ability has a relationship to their talent and their potential. You have to find the links. As I said earlier, look at what they do outside work, voluntarily. Look at the skills and abilities they have and use there and relate them to what you are asking them to do at work.

A persons job is not who they are. A sportsperson's sport is not who *they* are either.

I have, on a number of occasions bumped into old school mates. What is one of the first questions they ask? What do you do now? In other words, what job do you do? Who do you work for? What level are you at so I can gauge my progress against yours? This is yet another sign of our inherent competitiveness. A better question, if they genuinely wanted to know about you, would be 'What do you enjoy doing in your spare time?'

Know your people; know them and understand them. It will make coaching and developing them a lot easier.

6.5. Instinct in decision making

Earlier we talked about one of the benefits of coaching, either in sport or in business, being to prepare the coachee for those points in time when they are on their own, either playing the sport or executing their roles. A key element in preparing them for that time is in their decision making. Consider any sportsperson; where once they start, or the gun goes off they are on their own. How the match, game or race is going will determine how they think and what decisions they make to avoid defeat or achieve a personal best. They will, hopefully, take into account all the coaching they have been given and assess all of their options before making the right call. It may be that their coaching and experience combine to form almost an instinct for making the right moves, so that the process is not even a conscious one, which takes a given length of time; they may just do it.

We mentioned Tennis players who find themselves on the end of a pasting because the way they have started the game has been wrong and their opponent is somehow managing to counter everything they do. Eventually the strength of their coaching and experience kicks in and they go through the rallies and plays whilst they take on fluids and come up with a different game plan. What they have done is to examine the evidence. What shots is my opponent making? Where am I playing the ball, right up to the baseline or just too short? Am I making him move enough? Am I letting him take the initiatives? They will look for the facts, the actual hard irrefutable facts about the way they and the opponent is playing and then, once they have that data, they can start to build a strategy to change things around. In Tennis, sometimes, they have the luxury of time to think it through and the momentum in a game can shift quite dramatically, over the course of even one point, at the crucial moment. In Swimming, it's little bit harder to change things around, but still, the swimmer has to be able to try to react, otherwise it's a bad day at the office and a wait until next time to get it right.

Decision making, particularly in a pressured situation is something sports people become conditioned for. Whether it's 'pass or shoot', they make a decision based upon, what they know; their skill, their reading of the situation, their confidence and their coaching. Sometimes, it comes off, sometimes they fail, but the point is that they have been able to make a decision themselves and have stuck to it.

In business we have to try to reach a level of coaching our people where they can make that type of call. There is, quite often, a hierarchical structure in businesses that prevents people from making decisions outside of their remit. Often these involve costs and expenditure of some sort. The best we can do as coaches, in empowering people to take decisions, is to provide them with a clear view on what decision making is about.

I had a colleague who was put in a sort of Project Management role when a new EPOS system was being trialled. It involved him being on call in case of any queries. One particular evening he took a call from one of the Pilot sites, who were having issues with the performance. He consulted a technical advisor from the company who had written the software and the recommendation was that one of the two controlling servers was rebooted. This they could do remotely, so he gave them the authority to do it. He could at that point have deferred the decision upwards, but he felt empowered and wanted to show his bosses that he wasn't afraid of taking responsibility. The server was duly rebooted and it didn't come back cleanly, losing all that days transaction data. This was quite a big deal. So, what did he learn from that? What are the potential risks? He should have asked if the reboot didn't happen cleanly, would it affect anything. In short, he made a decision without all the facts available to him. Amazingly, he wasn't berated for it and there were positives to take from it. His boss actually articulated those and made him feel much better. The positives were:

- He made a decision without feeling he had to check it with anyone higher – Taking responsibility.
- He had checked with a technical advisor – Using resources.

- The system performance did actually improve, as a result, making the customer experience more acceptable – Measurable outcome.
- The risk of rebooting the server during trading hours meant that the process was changed – Mitigation of future risk

As a result, he didn't feel that he should defer all future decisions upwards, but should ask the right questions and get all the information he needed before taking them himself. The more decisions he made and chose correctly, the more his confidence and technique grew. You could say that he developed a nose for making the right call as his decision making seemed to become instinctive.

So at what point should we let our charges loose on making important decisions? Each will be individual and each will take as long as it takes. You have to judge, but a good way to start is to involve them in your own decision making, ask what they would do. Get them to articulate why they would take that particular route. If they are wrong – or you believe them to be wrong – explain why you would make a different decision. Make sure your reasons are factual and supported by evidence, don't just tell them that they are wrong. In the process you might explain why their approach might not work, but never, ever say they are wrong, otherwise you will break their confidence for the future.

There is one other thing to say about decisions. They should feel right. It sounds a little fluffy to say that and a bit glib, but if you have made a lot of decisions over the years you will know what I mean. It is that point where all the facts and evidence coupled with the need to make the decision are shouting at you to make the call. There is no doubt in your mind and you are confident that there is no better alternative.

Back to the sporting analogies albeit briefly; How many times in football games have you seen a player hit a speculative shot, often a snap shot, from a bizarre angle or an unfeasible distance? How often are those efforts rewarded with a great shot on target or even a goal? I would speculate, based upon discussions I have had, that those who miss, probably had that brief feeling that it wasn't going to work, but they were committed and hit it anyway; whereas, those who tasted success would probably say that *'it felt right'*.

6.6. Instinct in 'drilling for oil'

"If you want to find oil, you have to drill wells." John Masters – Wildcat Oil and Gas Driller.

The above quote is from a wildcat oil driller who has a lot of success in finding oil and gas. The reason he believes that he is so successful is because he just gets on with it. You can apply the principle equally to sport and business. Mr Masters' view is that you can make all the plans and look at all the drawings and computer simulations you like, but until you cut through the rock and actually find it, you haven't achieved anything. I believe he's right.

There are two schools of thought that go something like; 'The more you do, the more you will be successful,' and 'The more you do, the more likely you are to make a mistake.' The relentless battle between the *glass is half full* and the *glass is half empty* brigades continues, even in the speculative area of productivity versus procrastination.

We have though, hopefully by now, convinced you that mistakes are not a bad thing. They are part of the learning process and are fundamental to good coaching. If nobody made mistakes, we wouldn't need coaching or, more importantly, coaches. The key message to get across is that we are all about getting stuff done. Whether it is in a sport or in a business context, we simply must just 'do'. If we avoid it, put it off or are afraid of it, we will never achieve anything.

Being a tall person, sports where lower centres of gravity and great balance are key elements, have never been my most successful ones. For example, skating, either on ice or on rollers was not a skill I could take on easily, but the fear of falling did not stop me from trying. I found, oddly, that I was better on the ice than on rollers, but then, I was a decent skier, maybe there is a link there? The point is; it is all about trying. You have to take that first step in any journey and you have to be prepared to make mistakes. If you never try, you will never know.

As a coach, you might have people you are coaching who are reluctant to try what you have suggested. In sport and in business there is always that fear of failure or looking silly that can create a barrier. You have to get past it and develop the habit of trying new things. Only that way will you prevent revisiting the same phobias time after time.

Whilst coaching seven and eight year olds on how to execute a racing dive, there was an element of this. They needed to gain trust that what you were telling them actually worked and that it would not hurt. Even a perfect demo, by another swimmer, did not allay all their fears. What were they most afraid of, do you think?

It was something I puzzled over between sessions. I realised that failure, was the biggest fear they had. They really wanted to do it properly, but were afraid they wouldn't be able to translate what they had heard and seen into their own movements. My solution to this was to go back to basics. I set up two diving blocks and started on poolside in the other two lanes. I had them line them up in two rows and just got them to rapidly dive in then return to the end of the line for the next go. Each time, as they came back, I gave them a brief coaching point, such as, "Roll forward, don't fall forwards," "Push slightly upwards from your ankles as you leave the pool side," and so on. By doing it this way, they attempted a lot more dives than in the previous sessions and each time, had a different thing to think about. Once I was happy that they were happy, we moved onto the blocks and did the same thing. By the end of the twenty minute session on dives, most of the group were hitting the required standard and had probably completed 15-20 dives each. It was intense, for them and us doing the coaching, but it really did work.

My point is that the repetition, rapid and with small corrections really had them doing something continuous and feeling the improvement. Had we let them just try a couple at their own pace, it would have taken a long time to build that confidence and skill.

I once also witnessed a rather innovative training session for a county level football team. It started with the usual warm up and fitness exercises, but then became something entirely different and quite inspiring. The coach lined up the players on the half way line and he and a few others distributed about twenty footballs all over the pitch between the edge of the box up to about thirty yards from goal. Basically then, you had to run, on his whistle and hit one of the balls into the empty net. If you missed, you had to run a lap of the pitch, if you scored, you went back to the half way line and turned and headed toward the other goal, on his whistle, where another twenty or so balls had been distributed, with the same intent. If you were quick off the mark, to hit the best positioned ball, you didn't have to run a lap. I watched about ten repetitions of this then asked the coach what the purpose was. His answer was quite intriguing. He basically said that this exercise encouraged them to have more shots on goal and on target in an actual game. The stats proved it for me. He showed me statistics they had assembled prior to him starting this coaching technique and they were something like this:

Average shots on goal per game	8
On target	4
Average Goals Scored per game	1

He then shared the stats post eight weeks of that coaching, with the average taken over the same period:

Average shots on goal per game	22
On target	15
Average Goals Scored per game	4

The team were promoted the following season with a record number of goals scored for that league. The coach had the view that, the more attempts they had, the more on target they could achieve and the more goals they would score. Clearly he was right.

What is also interesting here is the proportion of each measure.

Increase in number of shots	63%
Increase in those on target	73%
Increase in goals per match	75%

Clearly, on these figures, more practice equals more accuracy.

In our business world, we should encourage people to try things, do things and get involved. To have a 'Can do' attitude is a strong positive and can be part of a work culture. If we continually coach it and make people see how productive it can be, it will benefit us all. They should not be afraid of trying to do more things, of coming up with ideas and suggestions. If you discourage people from doing these things by negativity, they will eventually stop doing them altogether.

One of the best ways to do that is not to criticise when things go wrong. Remember, as we said earlier, as a coach, it may be your fault that they make the wrong call or miss a target. You have to be a part of their decision making and endeavour and be party to it, not divorced from it. The football coach above encouraged the guys to take a shot, not berate them for wasting a chance or opportunity. This is the way you must go about it. In a business situation, we look for outcomes. We aim for very specific goals and results. We mentioned in an earlier chapter that if people know the goals and are closer to the intended outcomes their decision making is generally better and faster. They are more likely to be pragmatic and innovative in the face of an issue than they are unsure, indecisive or apparently, lost. As long as they know they will achieve the desired outcome, they will have the confidence to press ahead with their pragmatic or innovative solution.

It is, as I have said, what can be termed a 'can do' attitude and many businesses owe their success to developing a culture that promotes such a thing. What you have to guard against though is the 'can do' spirit being abused by those who want to circumvent your processes. Working in a business for a long time and being known as a safe pair of hands, is seen by some as an open invitation to operate a 'drive by'. These are instances when you are visited by the old, friendly colleague who comes up to your desk with the opening line "Would you be able to..?" or "Can you just..?" You know it's the pre-cursor to you getting a job to do, you have to coach your people to be 'Can do' types, but with some measure of control about how they react to it.

Some of the most productive and successful business people, follow a simple three point mantra; Plan-Execute-Review. They don't dwell on success or failure. They don't operate a blame culture or try to score any political wins. It is all about doing something and then getting on with the next thing. Sure, they learn from what they did in the review stage, but it isn't a post-mortem. No-one gets fired or lambasted for their performance, unless it is absolutely necessary. You will hear football managers who try this with an element of insincerity after a crippling defeat. Trying to insist that the 6-0 defeat at home does not affect the team and that they take each game as it comes. It is easy to say, but not so easy to do. If you can get into the habit of Plan, Execute, Review, then the results will start to accumulate.

What could go wrong? Something perhaps to be more aware of, than dwell on, is what could go wrong. If you are aware of it, you will be aware of why it may go wrong and therefore be in a position where you may be able to mitigate that occurrence. If you dwell on it too much, you may never get started and it will dominate your thinking. You will become afraid of failure, and we have already discussed why that is a bad thing. Sometimes by thinking quickly about what might go wrong and deciding how you may either avoid it or address it, once it has occurred, will allow you to move on and face the battle. Consider our Swimmer again. What if they get a bad start and are a metre or two down when they surface from the dive? They could put in a faster stroke. They could really focus on getting a good turn. They could, if it's a heat, just go for damage limitation and make sure they qualify. There is no need to panic when they find themselves in that position, if they have already thought about it, and what would work best for them. Similarly, a golfer, not playing particularly well that day, looking at a shot off the tee, may see bunkers to the left of the likely target area and a stream and out of bounds just to the right as the hole dog-legs. A slice or a draw would mean disaster. It might mean that the golfer decides to play short to the two potential traps and then play a longer shot over them to the green. It's all about assessing the risks and making appropriate adjustments.

In the final chapter then, we have looked at the main people involved in coaching; you and the people you coach. We have discussed how important it is to know yourself and what kind of coach you are. The circumstances and situations when you do your best coaching and, your worst, so that you can avoid that. We have also discussed how you should know the people you are coaching. People don't come with a manual, telling you which buttons to press to get the best performance. They are all different and unique and need you to recognise and respond accordingly. We have also looked at equipping your people to be independent and make decisions for themselves, based on what you have taught and coached them and their own experiences. In the process we have reached the point where their future direction can be to specialise or generalise. This is a decision they have to make, but where you can and should guide them. Finally we looked at decision making and the fact that your coaching should be engineering people to use their instincts and what they have learned to be able to make great, fast decisions. In that context, we talked about how 'just doing things' is a very powerful aid to learning and creating opportunities to be coached.

Next is a brief summary of this book and its contents. Hopefully it will remind you of where you were when you began reading and equally hopefully you will now find yourself in a different place, having been enlightened, coached and perhaps even educated a little, that, in business, we have something very useful and very powerful to learn from sport.

7. Summary

By now I hope that I have inspired you and given you plenty to think about in terms of how you coach, how Sports coaches might approach things and how you might adopt some of those techniques in the future. If you have a problem, try and align it to one which a sports coach might encounter and draw a comparison, it will help you to understand the issue and see it from an entirely new viewpoint. It will also help you explain it in a more memorable way to those who are coaching.

You could always try a little self development of your own and go and actually learn to be a sports coach yourself. I know of many people in senior positions who have taken up some form of coaching – usually because their kids got involved in a sport – and they all, without exception, say how much that experience has helped them coach in business. Let's face it, if you can get a difficult concept across to a child of nine or ten, it should be a breeze dealing with motivated adults. I also think, in that situation, you begin to examine yourself more closely and *that*, as we have seen, is important to *you* as a coach, your credibility and your disposition. Look at yourself in relation to the T.A.S.K. towers we saw in Chapter 3 and assess where you think you are. If you want to be a successful coach of others, try a bit of self help first. Look inwards at yourself and then from another angle. Try and see yourself as others do and define how you would like to be seen. If you don't have a particular view on this and say things like 'I don't care what they think of me,' you will never be a great coach. Their admiration, respect and loyalty will have a direct relationship to how successful you are and therefore how successful they are. Never underestimate the power of being a good solid role model. It is coaching without really doing anything.

So what have we actually done, if we have followed the programme and models I have set out? We have taken an individual or group with talent. We have recognised that talent and positioned it with the individual or within the team. We have then discussed how to refine it so that it is recognisable and tangible, before making it the best it can be. We have then looked at the science and art in coaching and how they are inextricably linked. We have looked at how to become a good coach and then how to become a great coach and what the differences are.

We have learned that the most important thing you can give to someone with talent and skill is opportunity.

The most important thing to take away from this book is that coaching is about people. Knowing them, understanding them, being prepared to help them develop and make best use of their talents is all part of the coaching you implement and practice.

There is one other indefatigable fact we can take from all the reading and study we might do on the subject. Coaching is about preparing people to cope and to use that as a platform from which to excel. It is about preparing people to think about the situation they are in and, sometimes without a great deal of experience, be able to find their way through it. It may not be pretty, the first time they do it, but we all learn from our experiences and perhaps one of the greatest lessons they can learn is, 'Actually, the coach was right.' Make sure you are!

The next time you watch the Golf on the TV or an International Swimming event, or even a Soccer match and you look at the competitors or players, try to imagine what is going on in their heads, before they hit that first tee shot, before the whistle blows or the gun goes off. They are there because they have the talent, the desire and the attributes to compete at that level. They are there because someone, somewhere in their past, gave them the opportunity to develop and excel. They are there because someone has coached them and brought out of them the very best that they can.

Now bring that kind of focus into your workplace and look at the people you coach or have coached. Examine their faces as they prepare to deliver a presentation, demonstrate a new product or address a Sales Conference. Ask yourself if you have prepared them to do what *they* do, with the same diligence, dedication, understanding and skill that a sports coach would. Have you prepared them to cope? Have you prepared them for that moment when they go, *off the blocks*, out on their own?

If your answer to those questions is anything other than YES! You are not a great coach, you are not even a good coach; you might at best be mediocre if you can answer yes to some of them. If you are committed to it, you might as well do it well!

Here is one final anecdote from me to finish off this summary and the book.

A friend and former colleague of mine once worked in a team with five other people. Four of them were, for want of a better expression, junior to him. Over a period of six years, each one of those four performed brilliantly and moved on to more senior roles, in other areas; two of them achieving Director level. My friend complained to me that, he was continually being bypassed by people he had trained and developed and that, *his face must not fit*.

I spoke with one of the (now senior) colleagues and asked them their view of my down-trodden friend. The answers were remarkable.
"What a great mentor and team leader, I learned so much from him."
"He made me what I am."
"There are some things he taught me I'll never forget."

These are great accolades and I replayed them to my friend pointing out that, all the signs were that he was a great coach and mentor. The fact that he hadn't been promoted, in the same period, indicated three things to me.

1. He had spent all of his time coaching and developing those guys and neglected his own development.
2. He had not made his success known to others nor had it been recognised.
3. He had not properly decided what sort of Manager/Coach he was going to be.

So what I would finally say to you is this.

- Coach and develop others, but allow yourself space and opportunity to grow.
- Celebrate and applaud your own successes. Don't wait for others to do it for you.
- Most importantly, decide what it is *you* want to be. What are *your* goals, *your* ambitions? Then go for it!

At the end of it all you must be a great coach to yourself, as well as to others. Practice what you preach.

Be memorable!

Acknowledgements

I list here the contributors of quotes and ideas I have used and drawn from in this publication.

Quotes
Napoleon Bonaparte
Winston Churchill
Dr John F MurrayFavourite quotes by and about coaches.
Steve HewittBasketball coach
David BristowWhen Milwaukee Brewers coach 1970-72
Lord Beaverbrook
Kurt SquireUniversity of Wisconcin
Doug JohnsonHockey Coach
Joey GallowayAmerican Football Player
John MastersWildcat Oil/Gas Driller

Publications
Kaye VivianWinning Proposals
Alain CordonCoaching d'equipe
Ken ColemanOne question
Edward De BonoSix Thinking Hats
Charles DarwinOn the origin of species